KT-225-218

PRAYER
FOR PILGRIMS

A Book About Prayer For Ordinary People

by
Sheila Cassidy

Collins
FOUNT PAPERBACKS

First published in 1980
by Fount Paperbacks, London

© Sheila Cassidy 1980

Made and printed in Great Britain by
William Collins Sons & Co Ltd, Glasgow

PRAYER FOR PILGRIMS

Sheila Cassidy was born in Lincolnshire in 1937 where her father, an Australian Rhodes Scholar, was Senior Lecturer at the Electrical Wireless School at Cranwell RAF Station. In 1949 the family emigrated to Australia, and in 1956 Sheila enrolled in the Medical School in the University of Sydney. Returning to England two years later, she transferred to Oxford University, where in 1960 she obtained a Second Class Honours degree in physiology. She did her clinical training at the Radcliffe Infirmary in Oxford, and in 1963 qualified as a doctor, working locally until in 1967 she decided to specialize in plastic surgery. By 1971 she had the Primary Fellowship of the Royal College of Surgeons.

Later that year Dr Cassidy went to Chile to gain wider experience in general surgery, working there as a doctor for just over four years. As a result of treating a wounded guerrilla she was arrested and imprisoned for two months. She returned to the United Kingdom at the end of December 1975, and has written *Audacity to Believe*, the story of her time in Chile. Dr Cassidy is now a novice at a convent in Britain.

This book is dedicated
in love and gratitude

to the Sisters of Mercy of Parramatta,
Australia
whose example first inspired me to pray,

to Michael Hollings, who encouraged me to
persevere,

and to the monks of Ampleforth Abbey,
who introduced me to the
Word of God

Contents

Once, long ago, I woke up
and found that I,
with all my foolishness, was a pilgrim.
Nothing else matters about myself.
This alone is of any importance.
This alone is my birth, growth, education.
I was
and am
afraid of this pilgrimage.
I am afraid of ravines and crevices in a land unsettled
and uninhabited.
I am afraid for my reputation.
I shake when others talk about me.
I am nervous and neurotic, but with all this
I am still the pilgrim, and, now and then,
at the right time, the pilgrim must
concretize his message. He must speak,
not that he is especially in the mood,
not that he seeks to do so.
Simply, the moment presents itself and he speaks.

Christopher Jones from *Listen Pilgrim*

Introduction

As I read the title of Sheila Cassidy's book and then went through what she had written, I found myself falling into the older person's kind of reminiscence. For me it was a pilgrimage backwards as well as forwards, making me rethink the years of coming and going with the Lord. From there I was led on to review my first acquaintance and then developing friendship with Sheila Cassidy, which is now coming of age in its twenty-first year.

Into my mind came the words of a hymn which she and I and others have often sung in the Catholic Chaplaincy at Oxford, in college chapels and in ecumenical gatherings. Shamelessly I would like to reproduce it here. Basically the theme is from the mind and heart of that great Englishman and author of *The Pilgrim's Progress*, John Bunyan. Here is the verse:

> He who would valiant be 'gainst all disaster;
> let him in constancy follow the master,
> there's no discouragement shall make him once relent
> his first avowed intent to be a pilgrim.
>
> Percy Dearmer, 1867–1937

Being an inveterate browser in bookshops, I find I come to my own criteria as I leaf through the abundance of every sort of book. When I am looking at a book on prayer and wondering whether to buy, I always look to see whether this question of mine can be answered affirmatively: does this author appear to write solely from an academic and cerebral knowledge of prayer, or from real personal experience as well? If the latter does not seem to be verified, the book goes back on the shelf. Many of us can write about prayer.

9

Introduction

There are fewer people who manage to live a life of prayer. Fewer people still live out a life of prayer, and then write about it. I can think of a string of names from the past. But where do we go today? Not so long ago, a Buddhist student at Birmingham University asked me: where today can I find someone who is teaching the kind of prayer I read about in *The Cloud of Unknowing*?

We live in all the hassle of the world, surrounded by extremes of riches and poverty, violence, starvation and over-indulgence, of doubt and disbelief. We need people who can speak to us from their living experience of all these multiple experiences, while not only retaining belief in God but positively growing in love and service of him.

The call of Jesus to follow, to live, to love and to serve is a call to listen to him in stillness, which we must make possible in our noisy, over-busy society. One of the beauties of Sheila Cassidy's pilgrimage of prayer is that she exposes the possibility of coming and going in relationship with God. For those of us who may have experienced a glimpse of God and then lost him in the fog and clamour of daily living, she presents a true and strongly encouraging picture. Some of us know with Sheila how God rediscovers us, often at the lowest point of our withdrawal, blankness and frustration bordering on despair.

The authentic message of these pages is the witness of an ordinary person struggling with life, enjoying and loving, suffering and coming through, but still seeking her way. As she continues, she looks with us at ordinary things – sea and birds and flowers and candles and people. Sharing, we can with her come through to a new relationship with God and the world, a relationship of hope, trust and love. The message of this pilgrim for all pilgrims is that we must be valiant, but not without fear; be constant in following the master, and accept the paradox entailed in all this of complexity and simplicity, of both the sublime and the ridiculous, indeed all that it means to be a pilgrim.

January 1980

MICHAEL HOLLINGS

Prologue

I like to think of our lives as being in the shape of a cross.

The upright – we can call it the vertical component – is man's relationship to God, his response to the first and greatest commandment of all:

> You shall love the Lord your God with all your heart and with all your soul and with all your strength.

This upright beam, then, is our prayer life.

The crossbeam – the horizontal component – is man's relationship with his fellow men: his response to the second commandment which is 'like unto the first':

> You shall love your neighbour as yourself.

Perhaps one of the greatest difficulties of the committed Christian is working out what is, for him, the correct balance between these two dimensions of his life. There is a very real sense in which we can never solve this problem because the more we pray the more we realize our need to pray, and the more we pour ourselves out for the hungry and the oppressed the more we feel called to serve. I have found my own answer to this problem, in so far as there is an answer, in a consideration of the mechanics of the cross.

Now, if a cross has a slender upright, the cross-beam it carries must be proportionately slender.

If we gradually increase the weight of the cross-beam, that is, if we try to carry a heavier and heavier load of social action on a weak prayer life, our cross will hold together for a while

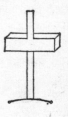

but there will come a time when the strain is too great – and the whole structure will buckle and fall. I believe that this happens to many people who are able to do great things for a while and, then, because they are running on their own energy, 'burn out'.

If, however, we make the upright of our cross

immensely strong and solid, if our prayer life is unshakeable and deeply rooted, then we shall find that we are able to support a broad and heavy cross-beam, that we can bear the weight of our brother's pain and suffering, steadily, day by day, because it is not we who are carrying the load, but God.

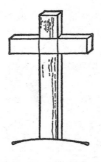

In Gratitude

I should like to say 'Thank you' to all the people who have helped me by commenting on various parts of the manuscript of this book: Michael, Anne, Colette, Gerry, Sister Dorothy, Sister Josephine Mary, Kate, Brendan, Christopher and Placid. In particular my thanks are due to Bon and Thomas and Aidan who spent many hours commenting on the original draft and in so doing made me realize how much had to be re-written. I am grateful once more to Kate Davis and Ken Fox for typing for an author who is always in a hurry, to Marjorie Villiers, my forthright editor and to Lesley Walmsley of Fount Paperbacks for her unfailing kindness and patience. Lastly, my thanks are to Pierre Collins for her very special warmth and enthusiasm which make all visits to my publishers such fun.

CHAPTER I

On a Personal Note

> I know only enough of God to want to
> worship him, by any means ready to hand.
> Annie Dillard, *Holy the Firm*

It was in my last year at school that I first began to pray seriously. Forced to repeat the year because of poor results, I was a little older than my contemporaries and became friendly with some of the nuns who were my teachers. Impressed by their kindness and evident serene humanity I wondered what made them tick and learned, to my surprise, that it was God.

Although my parents were Catholic my mother was a convert from Anglicanism who grew to dislike and despise the Church of Rome as she grew older. My father was a devout and punctilious Catholic who never missed Mass on Sundays or Holy Days but would have thought it excessive to go to church during the week. We did not pray together as a family and God was only referred to distantly as 'the Almighty'; Mass on Sunday was a dreary obligation, relieved only by the enormous compensatory breakfast that my mother cooked for us while we were at church. There was a curious incident while I was quite a small child that has, I think, considerable bearing on my attitude to religion in later life. One Sunday, when I was about eight, it was discovered on arriving at the church that I had forgotten my hat. Rather than take me into church thus indecently clad my father made me sit outside in the car whilst he and my brother went in.

I do not recall whether I wept or sulked or re-joiced at escaping sitting through a long service, but I know that I grew up with an intuitive certainty that if God was for real then he loved me with or without my hat and that I was welcome in his house in my ordinary clothes.

I have, of course, long since come to understand and respect the psychological motives that lead most people to dress in their best clothes to go to church on Sunday, but I retain my conviction that worship should be an integral part of daily living and not a once-a-week affair.

So it was, that at the age of seventeen I first met people who took God seriously as part of everyday living, and I found that this made more sense than a religion limited to brief night prayers and Mass by obligation on Sundays. It was in these sisters that I had my first important encounter with Christ and although I do not remember a particular moment of conversion I know that I changed from being a devious child who deliberately employed a chronic graveyard cough to be let off getting up for Mass, to a regular attendant at daily Mass and a person who tried to pray.

It is, as those who have done it know, both a marvellous and a terrifying thing to fall into the hands of the living God, and at the age of seventeen I fell.

About halfway through my last year at school I felt for the first time a calling to the religious life. This sense of 'vocation' both appalled and frightened me and, unable to come to any clear decision, I followed my original plan to study medicine.

In early 1956 I became a medical student at the University of Sydney. It was easy to go to Mass each day and to pray on a regular basis and, with the support of a helpful priest, I learned and thought about the service of God while throwing myself wholeheartedly into university work and life. These were happy days and I thought no more about convents until halfway through my second year of the medical course.

The Principal of the college was replaced by a younger woman of particularly strong personality and outspoken ways. We became friends and she talked to me openly about God and prayer in a way that no one had done before, and challenged me directly to consider whether God was calling me to give up medicine and become a nun. Thrown once more into a state of great anguish and indecision I was driven to pray with greater fervour.

When, the following year, my parents returned to England, I left Sydney University to go to Oxford and it was not without relief that I 'escaped' from the voice that articulated my deepest fears. I learned later, however, that one does not escape from God simply by changing continents.

My Oxford days were joyous ones and I continued going to Mass each day. I even tried to convert the world by starting a group to study the Mass.

The following year was a decisive one for me and many other Oxford Catholics, for Monsignor Valentine Elwes, a gentle and holy priest of the 'old school', was replaced by a man, twenty years his junior, who was quite transparently on fire with the love of God. Father Michael Hollings brought a wind of change to the Oxford Catholic Chaplaincy that altered the style of that venerable institution and had a radical effect upon the lives of many of its young members. From the beginning the chaplaincy was run as an 'open house'; Michael declared himself at home to all and we took him at his word. We came to breakfast, to lunch, to tea and to supper, and I suspect we ate and drank him into near bankruptcy but still there was a welcome for all. I became a regular visitor, first at tea time and then at the early morning Mass and breakfast.

It was here, in the old Nissen hut chapel, that I learned that the secret of Michael's strength lay in his prayer. I began by noticing that when I arrived early for Mass he was sitting quietly praying. Drawn instinctively to want to be with him, I arrived each day a little earlier, but however early I arrived he was always there. After a few months I made a point of arriving before he opened the chapel and would sit patiently on the wall outside the church until I heard the key turn in the lock. Unaccustomed at twenty-two to prolonged prayer, I found the half-hour difficult to cope with and would certainly never have done it if he had not been there. But he was – always. It was then that I realized that his time of rising was a fixed point in his life and did not depend upon what time he had gone to bed. There must have been many short nights for Michael in those Oxford days, for we kept him up late and he was not infrequently called from his bed by tearful lovers or those with other crises.

So it was that for the next five years, most mornings, I prayed for half an hour before Mass. I have little memory of how I prayed except that it was mainly in my own words and that it was often so difficult that I had to hold on to the chair to stop myself walking out.

My religious knowledge in those days was almost wholly intuitive. I developed a distaste amounting to physical nausea for spiritual books and for the next fifteen years the only religious book I could bear to read was Michael's first book on prayer: *Hey You*.

In July 1963 I qualified as a doctor and the following month began my residency at the Radcliffe Infirmary. From the beginning things were very different. On duty twenty-four hours a day, seven days a week, I was a virtual prisoner in the hospital; my days were long and my nights nearly always broken. Going wearily to bed at two a.m. with the prospect of being called at four, I had no strength to pray and, little by little, my prayer life disintegrated. Daily Mass was out of the question and even Sunday Mass was often difficult. At first I was concerned and in confession repeatedly accused myself of neglecting prayer, but found that I was unable to discipline myself to even ten minutes' regular prayer a day. So it happened, over the next five years, that I virtually ceased to pray and after a while I also ceased to care about it. Without falling into any grave sin I slowly changed from a devout and prayerful Christian to one who neither prayed nor went to church; slowly my values and ambitions changed too and I became totally immersed in my own private world of the battle for success in the medical rat race and the attainment of a better standard of living.

With hindsight, I see this change in attitude to life and people as a direct result of my falling away from the practice of prayer. It is this experience of falling away from God through lack of discipline in prayer that moves me to write this book, because I believe that what happened to me happens to many people. Overwork and lack of fidelity to prayer can be a destructive force in the lives not only of lay people but of priests and religious. The following chapters are born of the experience of the battle I had to remain faithful to prayer when I returned to the practice of my faith after an interval of over ten years, during which I prayed hardly at all.

In December 1971, when I was thirty-four, weary of long hours in the British National Health Service, I decided to seek further experience in Chile, a country where working conditions for doctors were better. Although I knew quite well that I was going to a 'developing' country I set out to work with the affluent professional class rather than serve the under-privileged and under-doctored poor. The events of those first two years in Chile, the difficulties of working in a strange country, the military coup of September 1973 and my gradual realization of the injustice which exists in Chile have been described in detail in *Audacity to Believe*. Suffice it then to say that those two years were both lonely and difficult as I struggled to learn Spanish and suffered deeply from the cultural shock of loss of friends, of ability to communicate and of prestige in my professional life.

The effect of loneliness upon people accustomed to pray is to throw them upon the mercy of God, but in 1972 I had virtually abandoned prayer and so took refuge in the escape from reality provided by novels and the company of my dog.

Then in March 1974 there came a turning point in my life. Consuelo, the Chilean doctor who had been my friend and whose house I shared, died. At the requiem Mass I found myself on my knees pouring out my desolation and anguish to the God of my childhood, and after a few days I returned quietly to my Father's house. Ten years is a long time but God is a patient and a jealous lover; as I resumed the practice of prayer and sat silently before him there came once more the stirrings of a calling to the religious life. After such an interval this took me completely by surprise and provoked the old reaction of fear and indignation at being called to what I saw as servitude. (It has taken me many years to understand that the religious life is in reality a call to freedom – but perhaps this is a truth that can only be learned by answering God's summons in blind faith.)

In August of that year I returned to England to see my father, who had cancer. During the six months at my home in Devon I spent many hours sitting praying and thinking by the river bank, for although the sense of calling to serve God in the religious life was strong, the desire to return to Chile was even stronger. In the few months between Consuelo's death and my return to England I had met a number of American missionaries who worked in the shanty towns among the very poor. These were priests such as I had never met before: men who burned with love for the under-privileged and with indignation at the evil which propagated discrimination and injustice. For the first time in my life I felt really proud to be a Catholic, for in them I found a Christianity that both frightened me and appealed to my instinctive yearning for authentic living. Back in the security of England I longed to return to Chile and work with them.

In December my father died and in January I returned to Chile, determined to work with the Catholic Church. By that time the priests who had become my friends had been expelled from the country for sheltering fugitives, as had Consuelo's cousin to whom I had lent my house while I was in England. So it happened that in the first few months after my return, afraid of getting into trouble, I remained relatively uninvolved with the poor. I found a part-time job in an emergency hospital and in my spare time spent many hours in prayer. I made frequent pilgrimages to a Benedictine monastery on a hill outside Santiago, the first part of the journey in a little green bus and the last half mile on foot. As I passed the lovely houses of the very wealthy I began to realize that I had reached a point of no return, and that I would never again be able to live at peace with myself if I adopted the comfortable lifestyle for which I had come in search only two years previously. It was a curious feeling: a combination of nostalgia for beauty and ease and cultured living, and a deep peace at my certainty that my own road was both narrow and steep. Perhaps I was beginning to understand the truth that the way walked by Christ is radically different from the one we would naturally choose, but it is one that leads through the Cross to deep joy and freedom of spirit.

As the weeks passed into months I made more and more friends among the missionaries. They came to my house and we talked and ate and prayed together, and I began to feel a part of their community. Then, in April 1975, they called my bluff by inviting me to work in the new church-sponsored clinic in the shanty town where they lived. Grudgingly, I accepted the invitation to work where I was most needed, rather than continue to compete with other doctors in the race for specialization, and in doing so took another irrevocable step towards involvement with the deprived.

At about the same time I met and began to receive advice from an English Jesuit priest. After making a retreat under his guidance I made a firm decision to return to England in the New Year and 'try my vocation' as a nun. Meanwhile, however, I threw myself heart and soul into my work and became each day more involved. My mind raced with schemes to help the people I worked with – workshops for the unemployed, better balanced meals for the children at the soup kitchen, the training of auxiliary workers at the clinic, and so on. Life now was very different from when I had first returned from England, and I travelled across Santiago each day, to work either at the Public Emergency Hospital or at the little church clinic. My trips to the monastery were now limited to once a week, when I would spend the day after my night on duty in weary and distracted prayer.

Aware that my work was consuming more time and energy each day I became afraid that prayer would become driven out of my life as it had been when I first began to practise as a doctor. Determined that this should not happen, I took stock of my day to see where I could fit in the hour of prayer that seemed vital to my survival. Realizing that the only constant free time in my day was the early morning, I forced myself out of bed each day to pray for half an hour before Mass, and when it was possible I also went to a nearby church in the evening. I learned, too, to pray on my way to and from work, and in the time it took me to walk to the bus stop, wait for the bus and make the journey to the hospital or clinic, I found another two hours in each day.

Once I began, I realized that there were endless

possibilities for prayer in my busy day. Praying as I walked down the street led quite naturally to praying as I walked in the long hospital corridors, and the discipline of praying in the bus was easily transferred to the time spent in the medical room when there were no patients to see. Little by little I acquired the habit of praying in the intervals between my work, and then of praying while I saw the patients. At first it was a deliberate act but after a while it became second nature to refer my problems and joys to God throughout the day, and to relax back into a more wordless sort of prayer when I found myself with a few free minutes to spare.

Although I knew that it was the prayer thus woven into my life that made it possible for me to give more and more of myself to the people with whom I worked, it required constant self-discipline to be faithful to formal prayer. I soon learnt that my ability to pray as I travelled or worked was largely dependent upon the half hour or hour given totally to prayer. If I let this formal time of prayer slip I no longer wanted or remembered to pray in the spare moments of the day, for it was easier to daydream or talk idly to whoever happened to be around. It was then that I learned the value of periodic withdrawal into the 'desert'.

An American friend, a nun, urged me to go and spend a few days at a house of prayer run by her Order. I protested that I was far too busy but she gently nagged me until I agreed to go for a couple of nights. The house was by the sea, about two hours' bus ride from Santiago and was run by two nuns who had felt a special call to prayer without being drawn to the life of the cloister. They lived very simply, dividing their day between prayer, reading and manual labour, just as men and women have done since the days of the Desert Fathers in early post-Christian times. There were two spare rooms for guests who wished to share their life, people like myself who needed time and space to relax and pray. Their chapel had been the living-room of the house and had two walls entirely of glass, so that on one side they overlooked the sea and on the other a pine forest behind the house. Each morning the sisters rose at four o'clock and prayed for three hours in silence and in darkness. At first I was too tired to join them but soon learned that praying by the light of the stars and as the sun rose made the early start and consequent weariness more than worthwhile.

After this first visit I returned many times and drank deeply of the peace and silence which permeated the house. It was there that I learned that to pray for five or six hours a day was not only possible but provided me with a strength and serenity that I was able to carry back with me to my busy life in the hospital. Thus I established a regular pattern of daily prayer, a weekly pilgrimage to the monastery for a period of extended quiet, and a visit every four to six weeks to the house of prayer. In this way I kept alive the flame of my love for God and tried to serve him in the people around me.

In October 1975 there began the drama that was to lead to my imprisonment and subsequent expulsion from Chile. At the request of a priest friend I treated a fugitive from the secret police, and a week later was arrested and interrogated. There is no call to repeat the story of my imprisonment, which is described in *Audacity to Believe*; suffice it to say that I was tortured for a number of hours, spent three weeks in solitary confinement and five weeks in a detention camp with over a hundred other women political prisoners.

On 30 December 1975 I was expelled from Chile and returned to the United Kingdom. My detention had aroused considerable public interest and indignation, and I stepped off the plane to a barrage of camera flashlights and questions from television and newspaper reporters. The disclosure of my treatment at the hands of the Chilean secret police caused a wave of publicity that took several months to subside. Instead of retiring quietly to the country to recover from the traumas of my experience, I found myself caught up within twenty-four hours in a world that was quite new to me. Realizing that I was in a unique position to give evidence on behalf of those whom I had left behind in the torture and detention centres of Chile, I gave many press, radio and television interviews. One thing led to another: a trip to Geneva to give evidence before the United Nations Commission on Human Rights was followed by a request to give a talk in the House of Commons. Then came an invitation to address a group of doctors in Paris, seminarians at Ushaw, university chaplaincies, Amnesty groups, and so on.

For over a year I travelled in England and abroad,

lecturing, giving interviews and meeting other people who worked for political prisoners. It was a marvellous but exhausting time and I was forced more than ever before to pray 'on the hoof'. I prayed in taxis as I crossed London, in trains and aeroplanes and always in great anguish before I lectured. Luckily, I do not find lecturing difficult but there is always a time of acute fear amounting to nausea in the half hour or so before I am due to speak; in the past two years I have sat sick and shivering in churches and cathedrals in many different countries, praying that the Lord would speak through me and that if this was the night when I should make a fool of myself, then so be it.

And now, the pattern of my life is different, for after two years of lecturing and writing I have found courage to follow the call to the religious life. At forty-one I have come to 'try my vocation' in a monastic house, to live out my belief that God is all in all. Where this will lead me, I do not know, and can only make my own the prayer of John Henry Newman:

> I do not ask to see
> the distant scene.
> One step enough for me.

CHAPTER II

What is Prayer?

Prayer is keeping company with God.
St Clement of Alexandria

The question 'What is prayer?' would seem at first
sight too obvious, perhaps an insult to the intelligence of any person who prays. And yet, when one
talks to people, it seems that there are almost as
many different ideas about prayer as there are
people who pray. The old 'penny catechism' tells us
that: 'Prayer is the raising up of the mind and heart
to God', a definition which is particularly useful
because it makes clear two important points. Firstly,
prayer is an act of the will; we deliberately choose
to raise or direct our minds and hearts to God.
Prayer is not something that just happens to us if
we are in the right mood, but a positive movement
on our part towards the God we cannot see. The
second point is that prayer is a movement not only
of the mind but of the heart. Prayer is not thinking
about God – it is our communication with him. If
our thoughts about God do not lead us to love him,
to praise him, to thank him for his gifts and to ask
him for what we need, then they are no more than
an academic exercise.

If we are to understand prayer as communication

with God we must look first at the way in which we communicate with each other and realize from the outset that it is a two-way process. Human beings communicate in many different ways: by talking and listening, by writing and reading, by touch, by expressions of face or body, by the use of music and art, by working or just being with each other in silence, and by the little-understood ways of extra-sensory perception. Our communication with God has many parallels with communication between persons. Much of prayer is just talking to God, sometimes in our own words, sometimes in the words of another which seems better suited to express what we wish to say. And, as in any conversation, part of prayer is listening.

When we speak of 'listening' to God we are talking about a listening of the spirit, a tuning of our inmost being to 'hear' the word of God. By 'the word of God' I mean not only the actual written words of the Scriptures but God's message in all its manifestations. God 'speaks' to us through the Scriptures, through the events in our lives, through the people we meet, through history, through nature – through everything. But, as in ordinary physical listening, we must keep silence if we are to hear what God is saying to us. Sometimes, of course, he will speak to people in such a manner that they cannot fail to hear – as, for instance, he spoke to Saul of Tarsus, in an encounter so violent that it knocked Saul off his horse and blinded him. Such dramatic Damascus road encounters are a part of our Christian heritage, but they are rare. Most people, like the prophet Elijah, find that God speaks very quietly. Elijah was told: 'Go out and stand on the mountain before Yahweh. Then Yahweh himself went by. There came a mighty wind so strong it tore the mountains and shattered the rocks before Yahweh. But Yahweh was not in the wind. After the wind came an earthquake. But Yahweh was not in the earthquake. After the earthquake came a fire. But Yahweh was not in the fire. After the fire came the sound of a gentle breeze. And when Elijah heard this, he covered his face with his cloak ...' (1 Kings 19: 11).

Just as Elijah recognized that God was speaking to him not in the wind or the earthquake but in the gentle breeze, we have to learn to hear him in the quiet of our soul and in the ordinary events of our day.

If, then, the voice of God is a gentle one we shall never hear it unless we learn to listen. We have to learn to listen in different ways and in different places: in silence and in noise. Perhaps it is because so many people have lost the art of listening that they have also lost the ability to pray. Accustomed to a continual background of music or chatter or traffic, we become uneasy when the noise stops and feel that something must be wrong. This is a sad thing, for if we live in the continual presence of noise we eventually lose the ability to hear acutely, to distinguish the elements that go to make up sound. We who live in the towns of this over-busy century have often to re-learn the art of being silent, and with it the art of listening. To do this requires effort and often we must take a journey, go away to some place in the country or walk by the sea and learn to be at peace on our own. If we do this quite deliberately, with the intention of seeking God, then we shall experience the wonderful transition of loneliness into solitude, and we shall begin to meet God in his creation and in ourselves.

In some curious way which is difficult to articulate, God speaks to us through the things he has created: through the sea, through mountains, sunsets, and, in a much gentler voice, almost a whisper, through things such as wild flowers and dried up leaves. But more of this later.

If God is speaking to us through people and through things we must learn to respond to him. Prayer is not simply a matter of asking God for what we need, though as children of a loving Father we must never be too proud or too frightened to ask for what we need. But prayer is a dialogue. If God smiles at us in a sudden shaft of sunlight then we must greet him in return, perhaps with a few words, perhaps just with a smile. If he reveals to us his loving laughter as we make fools of ourselves, we must learn to laugh with him. This is a hard lesson but a very beautiful one. (God has a colossal sense of humour – of that I am convinced!)

The Church, wise (if often exasperating) mother that she is, teaches us to use all our faculties in our dialogue with God. We bow, bend the knee, incline our heads and even dance to tell of our awe at God's grandeur, or to praise him. We sing with all that is in us to speak of our need, our sorrow for sin, our joy that he loves us. Those who can paint use pencil or brush to express their feelings about their creator; musicians write music, sculptors make statues, and so on. Just as longing for the beloved moves the lover to write sonnets, knit socks, bake cakes, give gifts, so we have a need to express ourselves in every possible form of worship.

We can pray, then, by talking to God, by singing a hymn, by making a movement of our body, by creating something in his honour and by simply being still in his presence, 'listening' to him. Slow reading of the Scriptures in search of God's message for us can lead to prayer, for it may be that a passage that we read sparks us off to make an act of love or praise of God so that we stop reading and just sit quietly with him. This slow and prayerful reading of the Scriptures has been used by men since pre-Christian times as a means of learning the ways of God, of listening to him, and of putting ourselves in a frame of mind where we can more easily talk to him or be still before him.

Closely related to this pondering on the word of God is what is known as meditation. It is often used as a synonym for prayer, but such a usage can lead to confusion and distress. It may be that those who find themselves unable to meditate are, in fact, being led into a different kind of prayer. For the purpose of this book we may define meditation as a deliberate intellectual dwelling upon some aspect of God, or of our relationship with him. The nature of the meditation will vary with the person who is making it. A time-honoured method of scriptural meditation is to imagine oneself to be present at some event in the life of Christ. For example we may imagine ourselves among the shepherds around the manger in Bethlehem, try to capture in imagination the atmosphere in the stable, feel the straw beneath our feet, hear the lowing of the animals, see the tenderness of Mary and Joseph with the new-born child. The purpose of this *exercise*, for it is indeed an exercise of the intellect and the imagination, is to *move* the heart to make an act of devotion to God.

Meditation, of course, does not have to be confined to scriptural themes. Practice and a fertile mind make it possible to use any person, object or event as the basis of a consideration which will move us to prayer.

If to imagine ourselves at the foot of the Cross on Calvary moves us to prayer of love and repentance – fine, let us meditate in this way. If, however, our minds become blank or we feel a profound distaste for this exercise, let us not feel guilty or condemn it but simply accept that it does not help us.

Another, perhaps more recent, use of the word meditation is for a form of prayer in which all words, thoughts and images are deliberately rejected from the mind. This type of prayer, which is common to many religions, will be considered in a later section. A consideration of transcendental meditation is outside the scope of this book.

This brings me to the very important subject of tolerance of other people's methods of prayer.

We are living in a time of great upheaval and

change in the prayer life of the Church, and there will be few Christians who are not aware of strong feelings, in themselves or in others, on the way in which both public and private prayer is conducted. Many older Roman Catholics are convinced that the fading use of Latin in the Mass or the Divine Office is a portent of the death of religion in our society. They not only mourn the passing of a liturgy they loved but they bitterly resent, as disrespectful and banal, much of the modern liturgy. This change in method and habits of devotion may be seen at many levels. An elderly nun may be scandalized that a younger one does not say the rosary, while a younger one may find herself quite unmoved by many of the traditional expressions of Catholic devotion to the Sacred Heart, the Virgin or the Saints. The same is true for position in prayer – an elderly person, brought up to believe that kneeling upright with the hands joined is the position of greatest devotion before God, may be horrified to find a younger person sitting cross-legged or even lying on the floor before the altar.

While respecting the feelings of others by conforming to the accepted norms when praying in places of public worship, it seems important to our understanding of the integral place of prayer in our lives to learn to pray in any place and in any position. We can address the God who made us with equal devotion while kneeling in the front pew of a cathedral or while lying in the bath. God knows our lying down and our rising up. We are equally present to him in church or in the bath and he will receive the cries of his children in any language and in any liturgical form. What matters is not the words we use or the music to which they are set but the state of our wills and hearts.

Let us therefore try to view our fellow worshippers as the Lord must view them. Let us be honest and say 'I can't stand the rosary as a devotion', or 'the way the Charismatics say "Hallelujah" and clap their hands makes me cringe', whilst realizing that our distaste is based upon difference of culture and temperament. We must not presume to judge the worship of our fellows, for only the Lord God sees into our hearts.

It is at this juncture that we can usefully discuss the question of feelings and emotions in prayer. It cannot be stressed too often that prayer is an act of the will and that whether we 'feel' that our prayer has been 'good' or useless is of no consequence whatsoever. If we make an effort of the will and compose ourselves to pray for half an hour, then, providing we do not deliberately choose to think about something else, we *are* praying. It may be that we will be filled with feelings of devotion, with sweetness in what we are doing, in which case let us be grateful. If, on the contrary, we feel nothing but our own aching knees and a sense of desperate boredom, then let us be equally at peace. What we feel at prayer is God's business, not ours, and we must strive to be totally abandoned to the presence of 'consolation' or of boredom when we pray.

A clear understanding that the value of our prayer does not depend upon how we feel is extremely important if we are to persevere in prayer. So many people feel that if their prayer is distracted it cannot be pleasing to God, and are therefore led to abandon their efforts precisely when fidelity is of the most importance. We are rarely responsible for our distractions in prayer and therefore, more often than not, in no way culpable for them. So often they have a human, physical or psychological cause. We may be tired, we may have indigestion, backache or any minor ailment, so that when we try to compose ourselves for prayer our consciousness is at once invaded and we find no peace. It is the same with those things which weigh upon our minds. A problem at work, a bereavement, a fear, an emotional upheaval, will inevitably invade the forefront of our mind. It is only when we consciously give in to these distractions that we cease to pray – if we gently push them from our mind and redirect our attention upon God then our prayer is not interrupted. The various ways in which the problem of distraction in prayer can be approached will be looked at in a later section – 'Problems in Prayer'.

Anyone who prays regularly over a long period of time will be familiar with the pattern of the appearance and the disappearance of 'consolation' in prayer. Here I am speaking of 'consolation' in a non-technical sense; about the feeling of warmth, of peace, of joy, of spiritual, emotional satisfaction that may come to us in prayer. It is obvious that much of this feeling is dependent upon our mood and upon the surroundings in which we find ourselves. To attend for the first time solemn Vespers in a monastery choir can be a breath-taking experience. The combination of Gothic arches, plain chant, the procession of the monks and the smell of the incense is enough to produce a feeling of devotion in the most hardened worshipper. And this is right and good. We are human beings and our physical, intellectual and emotional faculties are all God's gift. Just as it would be a mistake to think that prayer unaccompanied by emotional satisfaction was of no value, so it would be a misunderstanding of our psychological make-up to believe that, because sunlight streaming through a stained glass window moves us to love and praise of God, this feeling has no value. All things are God's gift and those things in his creation which move us to love him are most especially his gift, his revelation to us. The psalmist was far less complicated than we and was not ashamed to say that 'the heavens show forth the glory of God'.

It is in this context that we can usefully return to consider the cultural and individual differences in the things that move people to pray. It is important to realize that a service, a devotion or a work of art that moves one person to deep prayer may move another to boredom or disgust. There is much 'bad' religious art in our churches and on sale in religious shops; those who have a cultural background which enables them to appreciate good art have every right, artistically, to deplore the existence of such inartistic and sentimental work – from an artistic point of view. But let us be wary of criticizing the feelings of devotion produced by this sort of art in

other people. If a plaster statue of the Sacred
Heart, with a gilt dagger stuck through it and drops
of blood on a flowing white robe, moves someone to
tears of repentance for the way in which he has
offended God, who are we to say that this statue is
'bad'? We can say, in private, that we think that,
artistically speaking, it is in appalling taste and
makes us feel sick, but we must be tolerant of the
devotion of the other. (All this is not to say, of
course, that we should not try to elevate the standards of religious art in our churches and help
people to appreciate good design and non-senti-
mental works – but let us tread with respect upon
this mine-strewn ground.)

One of the break-throughs that I have experienced in the understanding of prayer is the signifi-
cance of 'wasting' time. One day I was working at a
boring job and a friend came to join me. He loitered
about for nearly an hour, perched on the edge of
the table, smoking a cigarette and talking occasionally of nothing in particular. When he had gone I
was filled with a special joy because I realized that
he had deliberately wasted an hour with me; it was
not that we were discussing something of importance or that I needed consoling: it was a pure and
unsolicited gift of time. If we think about it, for
busy people time is often the most precious thing
they have to give. Doctors, priests, those who counsel, will always 'spend' time with those in need.
They may sit up all night with someone who is distressed; they may pass long hours in listening to
problems, or in giving advice; but this is all time

deliberately *spent*. We only deliberately waste time with those we love – it is the purest sign that we love someone if we choose to spend time idly in their presence when we could be doing something more 'constructive'. And so it is with prayer: there is a very real sense in which prayer is a waste of time. God does not need our prayers and, more often than not, we will be unaware that we have 'received' anything from the time we have spent in prayer. It is because prayer is so often boring and unrewarding that it is the purest sign of our love for God that we are prepared to 'waste' our time with him; and it is only by wasting time in this way that we shall learn that it is not God who needs us but we who cannot live without him.

Prayer, then, is many things, but in essence it is dialogue with God. It is an act of the will and involves both the mind or the heart but not necessarily the emotions. The way in which people pray varies according to a multitude of factors which include especially culture, temperament, mood and the grace that may have been given. (For prayer is always a gift, as are faith and the life of the Spirit within us.) Prayer can be easy – but mostly it is hard work. It can be enormously rewarding – 'sweeter than honey, than honey from the comb' (Psalm 19) – but often it is dull and boring and apparently unrewarding.

Why then do people pray? Perhaps each person must answer this question for himself. Some pray because they want something of God, or because they are frightened and cry out instinctively for help. Others pray because they have been trained to do so since they were children and it has become a habit. Yet others pray because they find it gives them strength or consolation. Perhaps most of us pray out of a mixture of all these motives, each of which is an expression of man's deep hunger for communication with the transcendent. Lastly, there are those who, by tireless fidelity to prayer and the free gift of God, have come to an experience of faith whereby they know at some deep level of their being that God is the beginning and the end of their existence. It is this 'knowledge' that leads to the prayer of pure love and adoration. Man prays for no other reason than that God exists.

CHAPTER III

Why Pray?

This is the curious nature of Mister God, that even while he is at the centre of all things he waits outside us and knocks to come in. It is we who open the door. Mister God doesn't break it down and come in, no, he knocks and waits.

From *Mister God, This Is Anna,* by Fynn

The answer to this question is not necessarily the same as the answer to that posed at the end of the previous chapter, 'Why *do* people pray?' This is not surprising because so often we do good things for motives which are not wholly pure. We buy a train ticket not only because it is just that we should pay for the service we receive but also because if we are caught evading the fare the consequences will be both humiliating and unpleasant. The principle is the same in many of the charitable acts that we perform. Suppose we give generously of our time and energy in helping to run a church concert to raise money for the disabled; our primary motive, of course, is the love we have for the disabled; but our good works are generously helped along by the gratitude of the vicar whom we respect and the enjoyment we derive from such activity.

Why Pray?

When I first began to analyse my motives for doing good works and for praying I was surprised and humbled to find how mixed they were. As a young doctor I found it easy to be a willing fetcher and carrier of X-rays, laboratory results, notes and the like because I admired the consultant for whom I worked, and it has always been the same for me in matters of the spirit. I have been encouraged to pray by meeting some person – usually a priest or a nun – whom I admired and wanted to emulate. It is only recently that I have come to accept this pattern of behaviour as part of the way that I personally function. I no longer feel guilty because I am drawn to pray by the presence of certain people; I accept this as a form of discipleship. Just as God reveals himself to us through the beauty and the grandeur of nature, through cataclysmic events, through the pattern of history, he reveals himself to us through people. Certain people 'mediate' God for others; the person of Christ shines, icon-like, through them. This is a difficult thing to talk about because obviously it can be a subjective phenomenon and may be inextricably intertwined with a purely human love and admiration. It is perhaps easier to understand if we think of some of the gentle, God-centred people of our own day – Mother Teresa springs immediately to mind, and Dom Helder Camara, the fearless prophet of the oppressed in Latin America. I remember experiencing this phenomenon of 'touching' Christ through a person the night I went to hear Cardinal Suenens talk in Oxford. I arrived a couple of minutes late and the lecture hall, which held a thousand people, was full, so I was shown to the basement. For an hour I sat on a hard chair in a dingy room with perhaps a dozen other people, listening to the voice of a man I could not see. I came away with the sense of having listened to someone very close to God; I was determined to attend his Mass the following morning and hear him speak again the next night. When I returned to my college I told friends the talk had been marvellous, but when asked what he'd said I had no idea. I only knew that I had heard words which made my heart burn within me.

The phrase 'did not our hearts burn within us as he talked to us on the road and explained Scriptures to us' (Luke 24: 32) was spoken by the two disciples who met the Risen Christ on the road to Emmaus. I find that this image comes close to describing the 'God feeling' that I get with certain people. This feeling moves me to pray and is one which has strengthened and encouraged me to persevere in prayer throughout my life.

All this is not to say that we should pray because the people we admire pray, but it is worth trying to understand that men and women of deep prayer often have a gentle radiance that draws people to them. They are imperfect mirrors of the unseen God. If meeting them moves us to pray let us not discard our inclinations as hero worship, but thank God that he has revealed himself to us through mere men. We all of us bear within us the life of Christ and, we, clay vessels that we are, may be used in spite, perhaps *because*, of our weakness, as instruments of God. In the end, however, it is only by praying that we shall come to learn the most important reason for prayer. The truth, that our relationship of created being to creator of its very nature demands worship, is intellectually acceptable but unlikely to move most people to pray. There is, however, another facet to this truth: God is Love and he created us out of love. By praying we enter into dialogue with Love itself, we come to know Him – albeit 'in a glass darkly' – but this knowledge of love, of the Risen Christ, is the deep reason for our prayer. For it is in 'knowing' Christ that we come to love him, and in loving him that we enter into a relationship of discipleship with him. Then by the action of the Spirit we are born again and given that which St Paul begs for his disciples, 'Kneeling before the father':

> Out of his infinite glory, may he give you the power through his Spirit for your hidden self to grow strong, so that Christ may live in your hearts through faith, and then, planted in love and built on love, you will, with all the saints, have strength to grasp the breadth and the length, the height and the depth; until, knowing the love of Christ which is beyond all knowledge, you are filled with the utter fullness of God.
>
> Ephesians 3: 16

Through prayer, then, our own and the prayer of others for us, we receive this power of the Spirit for our hidden selves to grow strong. This is not a physical strength but a spiritual one whereby we grow in love, in patience, kindness, humility and self-control. It is the strength that enables us to turn from our natural inclination to centre on self and give of our time, our love, our possessions to others.

This is no magic formula, no instant recipe for holiness; but the more we pray the more we shall understand the truth of Paul's statement that God's power 'working in us can do infinitely more than we can ask or imagine' (Ephesians 3: 20).

God's grace, working through our human nature, manifests itself in this growth in the 'fruits of the Spirit'. Like all growth it is a slow process, it is aided by pruning that is always painful, and is often unrecognized by the person in whom it occurs. It is seen at its most remarkable in strong and wilful personalities such as those of Augustine or Teresa of Avila, but it is evident too in people of our own day and in ourselves. Sometimes it is clearly manifested in lives dedicated to service or laid down for love, but mostly it is a humble story of tempers held in check, of greed controlled, of hatred purified into tolerance and flowering into love. It is a question of pain or disability cheerfully borne, of menial tasks performed with fidelity, of brain-damaged children lovingly tended, of the patient living out of life in difficult, unchangeable situations.

God's gifts are special for each of us, for our needs differ and what he asks of one he will not demand of another. This is the miracle of grace: that the

Lord will always provide. But as the German pastor, Dietrich Bonhoeffer (executed by the Nazis in 1945) says:

> I believe that God will give us all the strength we need to help us resist in times of distress. But he never gives it in advance, lest we should rely on ourselves and not on him alone.
>
> Dietrich Bonhoeffer,
> *Letters and Papers from Prison*

We should pray, then, because God is our all-powerful creator,

> Thou mastering me, God,
> giver of breath and bread
> G. M. Hopkins

who holds us in the hollow of his hand. But beyond this unassailable demand for a worship of awe and submission is the unbelievable message, slowly revealed to the Jews in their relationship with the God of the Old Testament and plainly stated for all men by Jesus Christ: God is Love. He made us because he loves us. His only Son took on human form to show us how to love: how to be gentle and generous, how to serve our fellow men and finally, if it be required of us, how to lay down our lives for love. We pray in order that we may come to know this God of love, to become like him, to be caught up into his fire. Prayer at its deepest level is nothing less than a love affair between man and God.

CHAPTER IV

How Should We Pray?

Pray as you can and not as you can't.
Abbot John Chapman,
Spiritual Letters

'Lord, teach us to pray.' This cry of the apostles to their master has been echoed over the centuries by people of every creed who have felt within themselves a hunger for the Absolute. In our own day men buy books, go to lectures, make retreats, sit at the feet of gurus so that they may learn how to pray. And yet, when the crunch comes, no one can learn to pray except by praying. We can encourage people to pray, we can pray with them, invite them to join us in our prayer, but in the end, they will only learn to pray by doing it themselves. Having said this I shall nevertheless attempt to set down something about the different ways in which people pray, not so much in the belief that anyone will find therein a formula for praying but rather to show that there are as many approaches to prayer as there are stars in the sky, or people on the earth. More than anything I want to show that all ways to God are good and that we must walk the road upon which we find ourselves. But we must *walk*, we must reach out to clasp the hand of the God who hungers to sweep us into his arms.

It seems practical to speak first of three apparently different ways of praying:

– using words composed by someone else;
– using our own words, however inadequate they may seem;
– using no words.

I do not say that any one way is better than another. Who can judge which prayer is most pleasing to God? How can we know if he prefers plain chant to folk hymns? Do we believe he listens more attentively to the prayer of the enclosed nun than to the anguished 'God help me' of the alcoholic as he reaches for the whisky bottle? Who can know the mind of God? We cannot. The nearest that we can come to knowing what is pleasing to God is the message that is burnt into the pages of the Scriptures: that it is not sacrifices and holocausts that delight him but the prayer of a humble and contrite heart – the man who casts no slur upon his neighbour and who defends the widow and the orphan. Christ tells us without ambiguity that if, as we go to our prayer, we recall that our brother has something against us then we should leave our gifts at the foot of the altar and go first to be reconciled with our brother.

I would suspect that the majority of people begin to pray by repeating the words of a prayer composed by someone else and that most praying people use some form of set prayer all their lives. God is so mysterious, often so unreal to us that we may be ill at ease and tongue-tied when we go to pray. We find our own words inadequate, or we have nothing to say and feel a certain security in praying in the words of the saints who seem to have grown closer to God than we can ever dream of doing.

There are many beautiful prayers that have been composed over the years and used by generations of people in private and public worship: the psalms, the Lord's prayer, the prayers of St Francis of Assisi, of St Ignatius of Loyola, St Thomas More and so on. If the words of a particular prayer appeal to us, if they articulate for us the cry we wish to make to God – then let us use them. There must be no false humility or pride about the prayers we use; it is the movement of our heart and our will that matters, not the words that we say. We must pray as we feel best able to pray, whether it is in the solemn words of our forefathers or in the casual language of one of the many modern writers. It is not the poetic beauty of our prayer, the correctness of its grammar, whether we address God as 'Omnipotent Lord' or simply as 'Abba, Father' that matters, but that we turn towards him in love, in thanks, in sorrow and in supplication.

There are many books of prayers available at the moment, so we may readily choose one that suits our temperament and our mood.

The psalms, those poem-prayers of the Jewish people, must have a special mention, not just because they form part of the official prayer of the Church but because they have a timeless quality that makes them as relevant today as when they were first written. The glory of the psalms lies not only in their lyrical beauty and pure scriptural content but in the way in which they speak to God for man in every mood. The psalms of the persecuted are the heart-rending cry of the man who is sick, alone, captive or in exile; those of praise, the joyful thanksgiving of the man who recognizes that his good fortune is not a chance happening but the gift of God. We have much to learn from the psalmist who has escaped the deadening folly of taking his world for granted. He sees the elements, the changing seasons, the world around him and all its creatures for what they are: part of God's revelation, his self-communication to us.

The psalms have been the prayer of priests and laymen since long before the time of Christ. In our own day they are organized, with readings from the Scriptures, to form the breviary, the official liturgical prayer of the Church. They are sung or recited by priests and monastic religious communities all over the world and by an increasing number of lay people. A special chapter has been dedicated to the praying of the psalms.

The use of his own words for prayer is perhaps completely natural to the child who kneels confidently beside his bed and says: 'God bless Mummy and Daddy and Aunty Margaret; and please, God, don't let it rain tomorrow because we are going to the Zoo.' What happens to us, then, as we leave behind the simplicity of childhood and find ourselves unable to talk freely to the God we once knew as our friend and Father? Perhaps it happens that, while our own understanding of the world in which we live develops with schooling and general education, our knowledge of God does not keep pace. Our minds, that have long ago rejected the existence of fairies and Santa Claus, suddenly rebel at the concept of the gentle Jesus with a woolly lamb on his shoulder, or the grandfather God figure with the long white beard. Unable to address ourselves to persons who are no longer real to us, we fail to realize that there is an adult understanding of God which can be accepted by the university professor no less than by the humble peasant.

The transference from the God of our childhood to a more adult understanding of God can be an intensely painful experience, and there is a sense in which this transference is never complete. We try always to lay hands on God, to say he is like this, he is like that; but the truth is that once we have an image of God we are holding in our hands only a statue, an idol of our own creation. It is not within our human capability to know what God is like — he is totally 'other'. So it is that the agnostic is quite right to disbelieve in the man-made God with a long white beard, and it may be that his honest doubt comes closer to an apprehension of the truth than does the sententious certainty of the man who believes he has 'tamed' the Alpha and the Omega, the beginning and the end.

It is the wondrous paradox of Christianity that this devastating non-knowledge of God can and does live in deep harmony with a personal relationship with him. We do not know who God is, and yet we know that he loves us and that we were made for him. Our prayer goes forth, not to a human ear that may be distracted or displeased with us but to him who made us, who hears all, who sees all and who 'holds' us all in existence. This is why we may communicate with God in so many ways and when we do not know what to say the Spirit speaks for us:

> For when we cannot choose words in order to pray properly, the Spirit himself expresses our plea in a way that could never be put into words, and God who knows everything in our hearts knows perfectly well what he means . . .
>
> Romans 8 : 26

Archbishop Anthony Bloom speaks of the way in which the deepest and most primitive cries of the human heart can and should be directed towards God as prayer. There is no man, he says, who has not cried out 'Let it be!' or 'Let it not be!' – and it is the shortest of steps to cry, 'Lord, let it be!' I like to think of these cries from the heart, expressions of our hopes and yearnings, as arrows which we may either fire at random into space or direct towards God as prayers. If we are able to do this, and it is quite simply an act of the will, we shall find that prayer begins to become an integral part of our life.

I sit on a rock and watch the sunset turn the sky crimson while the sun sinks like a ball of fire into the sea. The pure joy produced by the beauty that I watch fills my heart and I cry 'Oh, how beautiful!' It requires only an act of the will to turn my natural exclamation into a joyous prayer of praise and thanksgiving and 'Oh, how beautiful!' naturally becomes 'O God, how beautiful, thank you'.

This conversion into prayer of our everyday joys, sorrows, hopes and desires is at first a conscious labour, but after a while it becomes second nature, so that converse with God becomes inextricably and wonderfully woven into the fabric of our lives. As we become accustomed to referring all to God, so our communication with him becomes progressively easier and more natural, so that we are often unaware that we are praying. Just, too, as people who are close to each other communicate in a sort of short-hand or language of their own or by a glance, so our prayer becomes less wordy and more simple. When I look with delight at the way the raindrops glisten on a gently opening rosebud I do not say: 'Dear Lord, that is a beautiful rose you have made; how wonderful you are and how good of you to give me the chance of seeing it.' No. Just as I would squeeze the hand of someone I love or share a glance of loving understanding, so I look at the rose and direct the arrow of my wonder and delight Godwards. And so it is with all things; the anguish and nausea I feel before preaching or giving a lecture will be articulated at most as a 'Dear God, please help me'; but this is my short-hand for a request not simply that I should speak well and not dry up in the middle of my talk, but that he should speak through me and touch the hearts of those who listen.

This kind of prayer comes quite naturally to

many people, although they often do not realize that they are praying. God is present everywhere. If, as the psalmist tells us, he knows our lying down and our rising up, why should we reserve our conversation with him for those moments when we go to church in our best clothes? This is not to say that we must not worship together as a community, for of course we must, and if it seems right, let us dress in our Sunday best; but let us not fool ourselves that this is all we owe to God in worship. If God is 'for real', if he holds us eternally in the hollow of his hand, then prayer is for every day and, in a greater or lesser way, for every moment of our lives.

As they persevere in prayer, many people find that the actual words they use become fewer, less organized, that they use them in a different way or that they find themselves praying without words. This type of prayer is not as mysterious as many people believe; it comes fairly naturally to some people and not at all to others. Like all prayer, it is a gift from God, for we would not be able to 'move' towards God if he did not first draw us and move us. This form of prayer is not a gift reserved for those who live in monasteries or enclosed convents, and many other people may find themselves confused and upset when their more formal 'methods' of prayer no longer 'work'. In this prayer 'without words' we make an act of the will and direct our attention to God, but we direct it quite deliberately to the God that we cannot know or see. We say no words, we think no thoughts and we conjure up no images; it is a naked attention of the will towards God. The author of *The Cloud of Unknowing* speaks of 'battering' the cloud of unknowing, directing the mind and heart nakedly towards the unknown God; we say no words of praise, make no effort to 'feel' sorrow or joy in the presence of God. We rest simply in the knowledge, in pure faith, that God is, and that we are. When we find ourselves unable to 'meditate', unable to formulate acts of love and sorrow to God, it may be that he is inviting us to be content with this 'naked intent', to walk unsupported by ideas, images and words, on the deep waters of faith.

This type of prayer is difficult to describe precisely because it has no shape, no form and no tangible content. It is a wordless, imageless, communication with God and perhaps has more in common with the deep unspoken communication between mother and child or between lovers. Let us imagine a mother sitting beside her sleeping child. She looks upon him with love; her whole attention is directed to him and she is, in a certain sense, at one with him. It is not necessary for her to say 'Sleep well, my darling' to express her desire for his peace, just as she has no need to articulate either in words or images her love for him or her concern that he should grow to become a sturdy adult and lead a life that is happy and fruitful. No, she simply sits, aware only that he sleeps and that she keeps watch with him. And so it is with God. We can sit with him on a mountain top, beside a lake, in a bus, in a darkened church, saying nothing, only being with him and for him.

Just as the mother watching her child may be filled with a sense of wonder and joy and sweetness in her love for him, so too our wordless prayer may be attended by a deep sense of peace and joy. But it is not always so, for as a mother, however deep her love, may grow weary and distracted in her vigil, so too our hours of watching may be invaded, unbidden, by boredom, weariness and countless distractions.

It is in this context that it is worth discussing how we can pray in different ways at different 'levels' of our being at the same time. Let us consider again for a moment the mother with her child; she sits beside him as he sleeps and as she sits she knits. One level of her mind is occupied with the very mechanical task of winding the wool about the needles; but at the same time, at a deeper level, her love and attention are fixed on the child. It is in this way that people occupied with a mechanical and repetitive task can pray while they are working. It is for this reason that monks deliberately occupy a part of their day with manual labour, for not only does this promote a healthiness of mind and body but such work leaves the mind free for prayer.

The same phenomenon is extremely common with certain rather automatic or repetitive prayers. Many people who pray the Rosary, for example, use the repeated Aves and the fingering of the beads as a way of stilling the active parts of their minds so that they can be engaged in a deep, wordless attention upon God. It is the same with the choral office. There will be days when the words of the psalms become our own and we are deeply aware of what we are saying, of praying in the words of the persecuted or of the man half out of his mind with joy and longing for the Lord. But there will be other days when the psalms will, as it were, flow over us and though we are singing or reciting we shall be unaware of the words we sing because we are engaged in worship of God at a deeper level of our being.

The use of the mantra, the repetition of a single word to still the mind and empty it of all thoughts and images so that it may be directed nakedly upon God, is another form of this type of prayer. The essence of this method of praying is that the upper levels of the mind are occupied in an automatic kind of way while the deeper level is concentrated and directed in the naked prayer of faith. The moment we begin to think deliberately, to plan, to discuss, to reason, the deeper prayer is broken, for we cannot deliberately concentrate on two things at once. In a similar way, a man whose mind is occupied in imageless, wordless prayer is quite unable to 'meditate' because his attention is elsewhere. What is possible is the free-wheeling, automatic, daydream type activity of the mind that may be repeating a phrase from a psalm, a verse from a hymn or simply be distracted by some secular matter. When I sit outside in the early morning to pray, I may be aware of the cries of the birds wheeling above me, of the smell of new-mown grass, of the cold wind upon my face, but at a deeper level I am praying, feeling nothing in particular, but open to the presence of God in me and in the world around me. An understanding of this activity of the mind at one level, while the deeper levels are engaged in prayer, is important if we are not to be made desperate by distractions at prayer, for it is often not possible to achieve a total stillness of the mind, and we can only renew our intention of prayer and our effort to direct our attention upon him alone.

The categorization of prayer in this way is deliberately simple, and in practice one form runs often imperceptibly into the other and back again. Most of the people I know who pray in this wordless way also pray the psalms and also use a greater or lesser degree of spoken prayer. The way they use the psalms may vary and the frequency of their articulated prayer will also vary. Private prayer is a highly personalized dialogue between man and God, and as in human communication the means used are not always easy to articulate. Each person will achieve his own way of communicating, depending upon his personality, experience and the grace of God.

Finally, perhaps we should think of prayer as an art which will only develop with care and perseverance and continued practice throughout our lifetime.

CHAPTER V

Where Should We Pray?

As thou takest thy seat at table, pray ...
As thou art putting on thy tunic, thank the
giver of it ...
When thou lookest up to heaven and gazest at
the beauty of the stars, pray to the Lord of the
visible world ...

> St Basil, from the 'Panegyrical
> Homily on Julitta'

The answer to this question is simple: we should
pray anywhere and everywhere. The Lord our God
is everywhere – with us in all places and at all times.
We are equally present to him at all hours of the
day and night – as the psalmist says:

> O where can I go from your spirit,
> or where can I flee from your face?
> If I climb the heavens, you are there.
> If I lie in the grave, you are there.
>
> If I take the wings of the dawn
> and dwell at the sea's furthest end,
> even there your hand would lead me,
> your right hand would hold me fast.
>
> Psalm 139

It is not God who is more present in a church or less present in a cinema, but we who are more aware of his presence in one place than in another. If we accept the truth of this it makes no sense to reserve our prayer for the time we spend in church; it becomes logical to advert to his presence everywhere. If the truth of this is at first hard to accept it is because we are conditioned to 'say our prayers' in church or at the foot of our beds at night, to keep our relationship with God in a watertight compartment separate from our daily life. And yet if we accept the logic of the constant presence of God in our lives then we must take our religion out of its Sunday box and condition ourselves to pray anywhere and everywhere. This 'conditioning' process is a perfectly simple and natural one that we can embark upon any time we choose. We come back again to the fundamental truth that prayer is an act of the will and that if we want to pray in any given place or circumstance we must make a deliberate effort.

In order to understand how we can learn to pray at all times and in all places it is useful to understand certain basic psychological facts about ourselves and our prayer. The first thing to realize is that we are restless creatures and that our minds are easily distracted from something which we do not find interesting. Now prayer can be totally absorbing, but most people, when they pray, find that the major difficulty is to prevent their minds from wandering away to other subjects. Many lay people look at monks or nuns in church and are amazed or envious that they can sit or kneel, apparently wrapped in prayer, for long periods of time. What they do not realize is that the person they are watching, and who is apparently lost in contemplation, is quite possibly desperately bored, plagued by distractions, or half asleep. What they are doing is behaving in a disciplined way, kneeling or sitting still, not looking around them: trying to be still in God's presence. In other words they are *trying* to pray – and because they are trying, making an effort of the will, they *are* praying. The lesson that we must learn from this is that if we are to learn to pray we must learn to discipline ourselves, to put ourselves in a physical and psychological state where we shall best be able to pray.

This brings us to another fact about the psychology of prayer: it is easier to concentrate our minds on God if we are relaxed and reasonably comfortable although not so positioned that we are likely to fall asleep. The position in which we pray is therefore important, not because it is more respectful to pray in one position than another, but because we are better able psychologically to dispose ourselves to pray if we are not tormented by a pain in our knees or an ache in our back.

Saint Ignatius of Loyola, in his *Spiritual Exercises*, tells us that when we begin our prayer we should try one position and if that is not satisfactory we should change it until we find one that suits us better. In practice, positions vary for people of different ages and cultures and in different places. In church, for example, if the kneelers and benches are well positioned we may find that we are most comfortable kneeling, or sitting with our feet on the kneeler and our elbows on our knees, and so on. In a small chapel with flat cushions we may find that the ideal position is sitting cross-legged on the floor with our backs free or supported against the wall. Lying prone on the floor is a marvellous position for feeling our smallness in relation to God, although it is, of course, a rather dramatic position and one that we can only adopt if we are among people who understand what we are doing. What matters is not the position we choose, but that we should be both alert and peaceful and free from acute discomfort so that our minds may be free to 'meet' God.

Just as we should position ourselves so as to minimize distraction from physical discomfort, so we should seek out a place where the distractions of our eyes and ears are also at a minimum. Once we have acquired the habit of prayer we shall find that it is often possible to pray in the midst of any distraction, but when we are beginning, and when we are free to choose, we are wise if we seek a place of relative solitude and silence. Once again this is a matter of temperament. Some people find themselves distracted by the slightest noise or movement and therefore are happiest praying in the solitude of an empty church or in their rooms. Others, and especially young people, are ill at ease with silence and will be more relaxed with some kind of background music.

Music can be a great help to some people in

prayer. This is very much a cultural and personal choice; whereas one person may find that putting on a record or tape of plain chant or soft classical music disposes them to pray, a teenager may be helped by modern popular music that adults dislike intensely. It cannot be stressed too often that we should use what helps us, be it bagpipes, Bach or the Beatles. The way we use music is also a personal thing; even those who prefer to pray in silence may find that if they are restless and distracted a brief period of listening to music helps them to relax and 'centre down' so that they can then turn it off and pray.

If we use music to help us to pray we must understand that this is an aid to concentration, a *method* of stilling our restlessness. We shall not be concentrating fully on the music but using it to occupy those restless superficial areas of our minds that would otherwise be running riot. It is obvious that if we are attending fully to the music we cannot be concentrating on our prayer – it is again a question of the different use of the different layers of our mind.

Just as music may be useful in stilling our imaginations and so making us more 'available' to God, so focusing our attention visually can make prayer easier. Let us consider how we pray in church: we sit or kneel before a crucifix, the altar or a statue, and focus our eyes upon it. Thus focused we are less distracted by the various movements of others in the church. We can sit, for example, in church while someone is doing the flowers on the altar. If we choose to watch her take away the dead flowers, wash the vases, arrange the new ones, then we are not praying but sitting in church watching the flower lady. If, however, we focus our attention on the altar and not on the lady we may be perfectly aware of her movements but quite uninterested in them and therefore undistracted. It all depends, not upon the flower lady, but upon us and what we choose to do with our minds. This ability to concentrate in prayer will, of course, vary from person to person and from day to day. One person will be irritated to desperation point by an old lady muttering her rosary at the back of the church while another will be quite oblivious. Similarly, there will be days when we can pray quite happily while someone vacuums the Sanctuary carpet and others when it will drive us out of the church.

Just as focusing our eyes upon the crucifix or a statue when we are in church is an aid to concentration, so we can learn to focus on an object in the privacy of our own rooms. It may be a crucifix, an icon or other object that will help us to recollect ourselves; another method which many people find helpful is to pray in almost total darkness, using only a candle to light the room. By 'using' darkness in this way they remove from sight the unwritten letters and other things which distract, and they create an atmosphere which is conducive to prayer. The act of focusing on the flame of the candle has in itself a quieting effect and helps to achieve a stillness of mind and spirit. The quiet and restful atmosphere produced by candlelight is also very helpful in group prayer, for people feel very much less self-conscious if they are sitting in semidarkness rather than under a bright central light. I labour this question of the use of darkness because of my own experience of the difficulty in praying in my bed-room and the way in which the use of candlelight has helped me. There is, too, some small sense of ceremony attached to the lighting of a candle which can say to us 'this is a special time for God' so that the very act of striking the match becomes the beginning of our prayer.

Another simple focusing technique can be of assistance in concentrating on prayer in different surroundings. Some years ago I accustomed myself to pray before a simple wooden cross so that the very shape of the cross was for me a reminder of God. I was at the time working in the emergency depart-ment of a hospital and when we had no patients I was free to sit in the doctors' room and read or talk. One day, as I sat there alone and gazed idly at the window, I became aware that the wooden pieces between the window panes formed a cross. As I sat looking at it I began to see the cross-pieces more clearly than the window frame so that it was as if I were sitting before a crucifix and I felt moved to pray. After that I began to look for the cross in the window and rapidly developed a visual trick of focusing on the cross so that it became, as it were, drawn in more heavily and the window frame and the other lines almost disappeared. From that time on I spent much time in that waiting room gazing at the window, praying. The room became for me a place of prayer because I had deliberately conditioned myself to see the cross in a perfectly ordinary window.

I learned to play the same trick in other places. For example, I had to walk down a long corridor from a certain office to the consulting rooms of the hospital; the corridor was L-shaped and at the end of the passage, before I turned to enter the emergency department, there was a door with a wooden frame and centre cross-piece. After I discovered the cross in this door I always walked very slowly down the corridor, towards the cross, rather the way one might approach a very beautiful crucifix in a church, so that this passage too became a special place of prayer.

By using such techniques we can learn to pray much of the time and take advantage of the odd minutes which would otherwise be spent daydreaming or talking.

Many people find that it is often much easier to pray out of doors. It does not seem important to ask why this is so, for we are complex creatures and our spiritual and psychological mechanisms are so closely interdependent that it is useless going to great lengths to try to separate them. If we find that the quietness of the countryside helps to still our minds or the fresh morning wind stops us from falling asleep, then let us gratefully accept these as God-given aids to prayer. There is, too, a natural sense of wonder and joy in the things of nature that we can 'use' in order to pray. The sense of awe that we get when looking at a majestic snow-capped mountain range or the peace that comes over us as we sit alone beside a lake can both be directed Godward so that they become prayer. There are some people who seem to be especially gifted with this sense of wonder in the things of nature; the nineteenth-century Jesuit poet Gerard Manley Hopkins wrote:

The world is charged with the grandeur of God
It will shake out like shining from shook foil.

From *God's Grandeur*

This appreciation of the presence of God in his creation is, like all things, pure gift, but it is a gift that we can deliberately dispose ourselves to receive.

If we go out into the countryside to be with God then we are much more likely to find him than if we go purely in search of exercise or the sunshine. It is often easier to be aware of God's presence in nature if we are alone and have the leisure to sit still or to walk very slowly. Simple preparations like wearing an extra sweater so that one can take off one's anorak and sit on the damp ground can convert a brisk walk by the river into an hour of quiet prayer. Those who sit still are much better disposed to notice the way the light changes in the sky or reflects upon the water, and so be filled with that joy that catapults them into a prayer of wordless praise and thanksgiving. As time passes, this sense of wonder can grow in the most marvellous way. Somehow we see the rabbits or birds each day for the first time, and the wild flowers have a magic beauty that is overwhelming.

I no longer worry whether this joy in the things of nature is a spiritual or a purely psychological phenomenon; whatever the mechanism their beauty moves me to pray and I ask no more.

If we make a habit of praying out of doors, of going out alone to look for God, without a transistor radio, or even a dog, it is likely that we shall learn to find him more and more. In the beginning it will be the dramatically beautiful sunsets or majestic views that make our hearts turn over. Then, little by little, we shall discover the wonder of very familiar things such as trees and flowers. The apprehension of the presence of God in nature, in all created things, depends not upon the beauty of the landscape but upon our own desire to see and our consequent heightened sense of perception. I learned the truth of this a couple of years ago when I made a retreat in an enclosed convent. Before I went I was convinced that I was going to miss the sea, the play of the evening light on the hillside and the freedom of being in the open countryside. To my complete amazement I found that being behind high brick walls enlarged my world instead of reducing it. I found myself entranced by the delicate workmanship of the fallen leaves and wandered about like someone bewitched, holding a few dried leaves and a piece of grass in my hands. I think I saw as much or more beauty of creation in the dried up leaves at the end of that hot summer as I had seen in the mountains of Switzerland or the beach at Rio de Janeiro.

This revelation of God in the things of nature is in no way confined to the countryside, although it is not easy to find the same stillness in the city; but if only we take the trouble to look and dispose our hearts to see we shall find God equally present in the heart of a town. It can be in the way the light plays on a railway bridge on a winter's morning, the glory of the Houses of Parliament floodlit on a summer's evening, or the way the sun comes out from behind black clouds as we travel across London from one engagement to another. 'Earth's crammed with heaven' and if we will only look we, like Elizabeth Barrett Browning, will see the glory of the Lord afire in every common bush.

God, then, is everywhere, whether we 'know' this in the darkness of faith or in that curious indescribable 'touching' that is his free gift to some people at some times.

The more we are able to assimilate this truth of the omnipresence of God the more natural it will become to pray to him wherever we are. If we make the effort, in faith, to search for God in all places then we shall learn the truth of Jesus' words 'Seek and ye shall find, knock and it shall be opened unto you'. It is this experience of the presence of God in all things that enabled the poet Francis Thompson to write 'In No Strange Land', a poem which speaks of the presence of the Kingdom amongst us:

O world invisible, we view thee,
O world intangible, we touch thee,
O world unknowable, we know thee,
Inapprehensible, we clutch thee!

Where Should We Pray?

Does the fish soar to find the ocean,
The eagle plunge to find the air –
That we ask of the stars in motion
If they have rumour of thee there.

Not where the wheeling systems darken,
And our benumbed conceiving soars!
The drift of pinions, would we hearken,
Beats at our own clay-shuttered doors.

The angels keep their ancient places,
Turn but a stone and start a wing!
'Tis ye, 'tis your estrangéd faces,
That miss the many-splendoured thing.

But (when so sad thou canst not sadder)
Cry – and upon thy so sore loss
Shall shine the traffic of Jacob's ladder
Pitched between Heaven and Charing Cross.

Yea, in the night, my soul, my daughter,
Cry, clinging Heaven by the hems;
And lo, Christ walking on the water,
Not of Gennesareth but Thames.

Francis Thompson

CHAPTER VI

When Should We Pray?

Ought we to pray without ceasing? Is it possible
to obey such a command? ... I will endeavour
to the best of my ability, to defend the charge.
St Basil, 'Panegyrical Homily on Julitta',
from *Heart of the Saints*, by Francis W. Johnston

St Paul tells us quite simply that we should pray at
all times:

Be joyful and pray at all times, be thankful
in all circumstances. This is what God wants
from you in your life in union with Christ
Jesus.

1 Thessalonians 5: 16–18

The words are clear enough, but somehow we are
inclined to pass them off as just another of those
completely absurd and impractical demands that
are to be found scattered throughout the New Testament: that we should love our enemies, turn the
other cheek to the man who strikes us, give our
cloak to the thief who steals our coat, deliberately
take the lowest place and so on. At first sight this
seems a philosophy of life that no one in their right
mind, least of all Christ himself, could expect us
to take seriously.

And yet, once we enter upon the path of Christian discipleship we discover, at first to our horror and then with a kind of joyous dread, that the gospels mean what they say; that this is the code of behaviour, the way of life, laid down for those who freely choose to follow Christ, to be Christians. We discover the awesome truth that those who strive to follow him must take up their cross each day, that they must die as the grain of wheat dies if they are to bear fruit, and that it is only in losing their lives for the sake of the Kingdom that they will ever begin to taste of the fullness of the life for which they were created.

So the Gospel is a demanding message which calls us to a way of life 'costing not less than everything' (T. S. Eliot, *Little Gidding*), and precisely because it is so difficult we cannot expect to journey this way without a guide, without the support of constant communication with God, without constant prayer.

As in all matters of the spirit, there is no magic formula, no technique we can learn, no machine we can buy that will make unceasing prayer an instant possibility. And yet if we seek courageously and honestly, with dogged perseverance and all the fidelity of which we are capable, we shall find that the impossible becomes possible, that our communication with God, hitherto limited to set times and places, can permeate all areas of our life. With this added dimension to our prayer comes an increasing awareness, albeit intermittent, of the presence of God in all things. Such awareness is mostly a matter of faith, of a mysterious 'knowing' without knowing, a 'seeing' without seeing, of 'touching' without feeling; and yet, if we make this movement of the will in blind faith towards God, we shall be given sufficient assurance of his presence with us for us to persevere in the practice of prayer.

Again, as in all matters of the spirit, this search for constant communication with God is a crazy mixture of the mystical and the mundane. Because our apprehension of the Absolute is a supernatural phenomenon we have no language to describe our experience and must therefore use words which only partially convey the truth we wish to share. The language of our meeting with God is much closer to the language of poets and lovers than that of scientists, for it is a language of imagery and parables and of words that have many meanings. So it happens that I can speak of 'experiencing' the presence of God as I sit huddled in the cold on a muddy river bank at half past six on an October morning.

How does it happen? Like any other mortal I am summoned rudely from my sleep by an alarm clock; I groan, I feel the anguish of unnatural awakening, the resentment at being woken, the overwhelming desire to go back to sleep. Perhaps for several minutes I lie with my head under the blankets saying to myself: 'This is nonsense. You need the sleep. It is far too cold. You can pray later on.' Then there comes the other voice within me which says: 'Go on. You know perfectly well that if you don't get up now the day will slip by without your praying.' Somehow I force myself out of bed, struggle into my clothes and, torch in hand, stumble out into the darkness of the garden.

Down by the river the world is beginning to emerge, bathed in a cold grey light, and I spread my anorak on the bank and sit down.

> O God, early in the morning I cry to you.
> Help me to pray
> And to concentrate my thoughts on you;
> I cannot do this alone.
> In me there is darkness ...
> > Dietrich Bonhoeffer, *Letters & Papers*
> > *From Prison*, The Enlarged Edition

I look at my watch: it is a quarter to seven, an hour and a quarter to breakfast. The time stretches before me like an eternity and I feel a desolate emptiness of body and spirit ...

What do I write now? How does one account for time 'wasted' in prayer? How can one remember how one prayed – three years ago, a year ago, this morning? In many ways each man's prayer is a mystery, not only to others but to himself. And yet, because the life of the Spirit is a discipleship and because we are all members of a community, a body, a family, we must try to share our experience if it is possible that in so doing we shall give encouragement and support to others.

My hours of prayer on the river bank near my home are not essentially different from those spent on a mountainside in Chile, in a parish church in London, or sitting overlooking a valley in Yorkshire. There is always the struggle to get up, the urge to go back to bed. Sometimes an hour seems incredibly long and I look at my watch a dozen times, conscious only of boredom and distraction and wanting my breakfast. Then there are the days when the early morning is filled with magic and the swirling mist over the valley is the pillar of cloud that barely conceals the unknowable, untouchable, the Alpha of my being. Sometimes my head is full of cotton, hay and rags, and I pray in stumbling disconnected words; other days a phrase from a psalm repeats itself in some distant part of my mind like waves lapping the edge of a lake. Some days I cannot drive the world, the flesh and the devil from me, and I know that I am no better than my ancestors. And yet on others I feel that I am touching what no hand has ever touched, seeing what no eye has ever seen. But however it goes, gazing at the sunrise or sitting in a cold church, in deep joy or in empty boredom, there is the knowledge that somehow, in a way that I cannot articulate to my own or anyone else's satisfaction, I am in communication with my God.

And so it goes on; every morning, more or less. Sometimes more, sometimes less, some days not at all. But the pattern is there, a pattern of fidelity that is fundamental to my survival as a follower of Christ.

Just as a man's relationship with his wife, a mother's with her children, is compounded of highs and lows, of peaks of intense love and valleys of despondency, with miles and miles of the flat land of ordinary living in between, so our relationship with God is a mixture of elation, depression and boredom. Precisely because the moments of joy and ecstasy are few and far between, the basis of our relationship must be a dogged fidelity to daily prayer. A mother's love for her family is expressed not only in the moments experienced by all as love, but also in the daily routine of washing, cleaning and cooking.

And so it is with prayer. Man's deep love of God can be expressed poetically in a hundred different ways.

> O God, you are my God, for you I long
> for you my soul is thirsting.
> My body pines after you,
> Like a dry, weary land without water.
> From Psalm 63

But it is lived out as a daily routine of prayer in which more often than not there is no comfort and no consolation. But just as the daily routine of cooking and caring is utterly vital to maintain the relationship between man and wife – without washed shirts and emptied dustbins there could be no twilight evenings and no roses – so without fidelity to prayer in boredom and dryness there can be no touching of the Absolute, no glimpse of Heaven in a wild flower.

If then we wish for a relationship with God that will pervade every aspect of our lives, take us over and transform us, we must learn to pray each day on a regular basis. Anyone who has attempted to make prayer an integral part of his life will know that it cannot be done without discipline.

In these days of informality and the search for personal freedom it is not fashionable to talk about discipline. Indeed, perhaps it is a need that each person can only learn for himself. One of the great truths that we must all learn is that without self-discipline we shall never be free, and that the more we learn to control ourselves the freer we become.

Imprisonment has led me to think much about the concepts of slavery and freedom, of oppression and liberation, and to understand that of all the factors militating against my freedom the most important of them by far are within me. I am not the person I would like to be, not because of the circumstances of my life or the society in which I live, but because of my own personal weaknesses of greed, selfishness and sloth. I am not as slim as I would wish because I eat too much, not as cultured as I would like because I do not make the time to read, and not the Christian I long to be because I am too selfish to give enough time and energy to God and to my neighbour.

It is important to be rigorous in this matter of finding time for prayer because it is so easy to fool oneself that one has no time, and so to miss out on the whole glorious reason for human existence. If we do not discipline ourselves to pray in a regular way every day we shall never allow our lives to be invaded by God, never achieve that openness to the Spirit that leads to an ever-increasing awareness of his presence in our lives and in the world around us. Conversely, if we have faith enough to realize our need for regular prayer, and courage to persevere, then we shall be open to receive a very precious gift of God: a condition of heart and spirit in which an awareness of God's presence is never far from our level of consciousness, so that we advert to his presence frequently, naturally and joyfully.

But how is this done? How can the busy man in the street or woman in her home find time for more than a few moments of snatched prayer beside the bed at night or half an hour at church on Sunday? Prayer is all very well, we may say, for nuns and monks – their whole life is geared to worship – but ordinary people cannot be expected to pray in this way.

It is certainly true that life in a monastery is (or should be) especially ordered to provide optimal conditions for continual prayer, but it is equally true that it is possible for most Christians to give more time to prayer than they do. We shall learn the truth of this not from books, but from the experience of trying to pray whilst working or playing, wherever we are. We shall learn by trial and error, by repeated failure and innumerable painful new beginnings.

The most important thing to be learned about finding time for prayer is that it depends not on the organization of time but on the attitude of mind. Most of us think of prayer as an important optional extra in life. When all things are equal, when the going is good, we pray regularly. But when work becomes too heavy or social life too demanding, prayer time is sacrificed. Our prayer occupies a peripheral position in our lives, and when the centre becomes overcrowded it is pushed out. The breakthrough comes when we realize that we have our priorities completely wrong and that we must make our relationship with God the axis of our life, the centre point around which all else revolves. Prayer must be the last thing to go when things get tight, not the first.

Once we look at our lives in this light, all things fall into perspective. When we are too busy we must give up recreation time, study time, meal times, sleep – all – before we allow our prayer time to be invaded. Now, having just written this I must at once admit that although this is the ideal I set myself, the pattern of life I strive to live, I do not always achieve it. In spite of my failure, however, I set it out because I know from the times when I *do* live up to it that it is possible. Not only is it possible, but it is a way of living which leads to a fullness of being unattainable in any other way. I am completely convinced that the half hour or hour that I give to prayer at the expense of my work or my leisure is time that is never wasted. In a way that I do not fully understand my work is more productive and my leisure more joyful when I have spent time with God. Prayer, even more than eating or sleeping, is not a luxury but a necessity, and we are only fully human when we remember this and arrange our life accordingly.

Given, then, the necessity for regular prayer, how

and when are we to fit it into our already over-full lives? This practical working out must clearly be a personal matter and will depend upon the sort of people we are, the lives we lead and the work we do. A pattern that will work for a married person is likely to be different from that suitable for a single man or woman, and the way for a teenager unlike that for the elderly. But the principle is the same for all: we must make prayer our first priority and arrange the rest of our lives accordingly.

Once one is convinced of the necessity for regular daily prayer it is simply a question of examining the structure of one's day to find what time is available. This must be a ruthlessly honest procedure, for it is all too easy to say and believe that one's day is completely full. For those who are not married the first 'place' to look for time is the early morning. We must examine the hour we get up, the time we go to bed and the number of hours we sleep. Many people deceive themselves about the amount of sleep they need, just as many are mistaken about the amount of food they need. One person will say 'I need nine hours', while another will be certain that he needs ten. Most adults, in fact, manage very well on seven hours with an occasional long sleep. There are people who seem to get by with as little as five hours – it is an individual matter. (Children and adolescents need more sleep than adults, a point to be borne in mind when one is helping generous and enthusiastic young people to make their lives prayer-centred.)

Let us look first of all, therefore, at the time we get up and see if we could not set our alarm half an hour, or even an hour, earlier. The early morning is for many people the best time to pray. There is a certain stillness of the mind before it has been invaded by the cares of the day that makes it easier to be quiet before God. It is not without reason that those in monastic orders rise early in the morning; generations of men and women have found that this is a good time to pray. Apart from the psychological aspects, praying early in the day has the great practical advantage that the rest of the world is in bed and one can be fairly certain that there will be no interruptions. There is too the fact that if one prays before the day's labour begins one can go forward in the knowledge that this important 'work' has been accomplished. If we leave our formal prayer time until the evening there will almost certainly be interruptions and calls upon our time that will militate against our fidelity.

If we are already rising early because we have a long journey to work it is still worth a look at our time of retiring. It may be that we are going to bed later than we need because we allow ourselves to be mesmerized by the television or sit up late talking. This last situation is especially true of undergraduates who, rightly rejoicing in the new freedom of university life, find it difficult to discipline themselves.

Early morning rising, although usually suitable for the single man or woman, can be difficult for those who are married, especially if only one partner is interested in praying in a serious way. It would obviously be destructive to a relationship if one member insisted on getting up an hour before the other. A married woman in particular will often find that the most peaceful time comes later in the day when she has got her husband off to work and her children to school. It is obviously important to be considerate of those with whom we live, and not to be so obtrusive in our demands for prayer time that it becomes a cause of conflict. There may well be a need for a combination of discretion, tact and honesty if the reorganization of life required is going to affect the household in any way. A typical situation is that of a busy schoolmaster who did not have a moment to himself from the time he got up until his school closed at four p.m. He was convinced that even a quarter of an hour of private prayer was quite impossible in his situation. Examining his day, however, it emerged that school closed at four and that he went home for his tea at a quarter past, driving past his parish church. It did not seem unreasonable that he should stop off regularly for fifteen minutes each day, thus arriving home for tea at half past four.

I have rather laboured this particular point because so many people are genuinely convinced that they have no time to pray, until they examine their daily timetable in this way.

Once we have established a routine of, say, fifteen or thirty minutes a day for private prayer we can start looking for other 'spaces' in our day so that we can increase our prayer time. If this seems peculiar I can only say that it is a fact that the more we pray the more we find that we need to pray, and the less we pray the less we realize our need to spend time with God in this way. Once we have begun to take prayer seriously we shall find that it becomes second nature to us to advert to God at various times during the course of the day, so that prayer becomes inextricably woven into the fabric of our life.

As our days become fuller and it is increasingly difficult to be certain of finding the time we need for prayer, we must look for the 'spaces' in our day. An example of such a 'space' is the time spent in travelling to work. We can determine to spend this time in prayer, and from the moment we step into the bus or train or car until the time we get out we can deliberately direct our minds towards God. The type of prayer that is possible varies with the conditions of our travelling. On a bus that is nearly empty it may be possible to be as recollected as if in one's own room or in a church. Travelling in the rush hour, of course, is a different matter. Wedged between two fat ladies in the centre of a bus on a summer afternoon it is not easy to give oneself to deep prayer. Even so, working on the principle of 'pray as you can and not as you can't' we can use our 'distractions' to pray. We can offer our discomfort as the only gift we have, pray for the patience to smile at fellow passengers, and for the grace to forgive those who tread on our toes or pick our pocket. Most of all we may 'give' those we meet to God – the mother with a young baby, the frail old lady, the school children, the lovers and all the others. We can try to look upon everyone with love, not emotional love, for that would be impossible, but with a love of the will. We can wish each one well and pray to God to hold him in his love.

There are, of course, many other ways in which we can work to weave prayer into our everyday lives. Some say a brief prayer when they pass a church or if someone swears at work; others carry a rosary in their pockets and pray as they walk or ride to work; many people now pray the psalms and make time to pray several times in the course of the day. The method we employ will depend upon our temperament and the type of lives we live, and the degree of recollection we achieve will depend not only upon the efforts we make but upon the gift of God. Some people are graced with a powerful sense of the presence of God in the world about them while others must live for years in blind faith. We have only to read St Thérèse of Lisieux's account of her years of doubt as to the existence of God to realize that all consolation in prayer is God's gift and that he may remove it from his most faithful and loving servants.* We must not therefore expect that a life of constant prayer will be an easy one – it may be extremely difficult – but dryness and doubt notwithstanding, a deepening relationship with God is the pathway to ever-increasing peace of soul and spiritual joy, and an essential element in deepening this relationship is prayer.

---

* *Autobiography of a Saint: Thérèse of Lisieux*, Ronald Knox (trans.).

CHAPTER VII

Praying in the Market Place

We shall never be safe in the market place unless we are at home in the desert.

Cardinal Basil Hume, O.S.B.,
Searching for God

The life of Christian discipleship is one of a constant tension between 'desert' and 'market place'. 'Desert' in this context means a place where we can withdraw to be alone with God. In practical terms this may mean a monastery, a retreat house, the nearest stretch of countryside where we can be alone, or simply the privacy of our rooms. The essence of the desert is that one is alone and therefore exposed to the silence of God, that scary creative silence that provides the optimal conditions for a man's encounter with his maker. The 'market place' is, quite simply, where the people are, where life throbs and where the cries of the joyous and the desolate fill the air. Here we meet with God incarnate, God made man, made you, made me, made neighbour. God is everywhere; his glory fills the desert and he walks beside us in the market place. We must find him wherever we go but, because we are creatures, we must accept that we shall find him in different ways at different times and in different places. The tension between the call to the desert and to the market place arises not from the greater presence of God in one or the other but from our varying psychological needs to apprehend him in different ways.

An understanding of this tension in ourselves and the acceptance of it as an integral part of life is of fundamental importance in achieving that vital peace of soul without which life becomes a torment. When we dwell in the desert we live with the painful awareness of the sick in need of a doctor, of the imprisoned in need of a liberator, of the indifferent in need of awakening. And yet when, made desperate by the cries of those who need our help, any man's help, we leave the desert and go into the market place, it is not long before we find that both our desire and our power to serve have been generated in the periods of aloneness and silence. Desert or market place, it is not a question of pitching our tent in one or the other, but of learning to go forth and withdraw as the needs of our brother and the needs of our spirit demand.

Most of us will spend our time in an attempt to resolve this tension within ourselves and this is good for, properly understood, it is the creative force which makes Christian discipleship possible. What we must learn, and it is the work of a lifetime, is to carry with us back to the market place the faith and strength that we find in the desert. We must carry back the live coals from our camp fire not only in order that we may survive but so that others may warm themselves at our hearth.

How then are we to keep our fire alive? Jostled and jostling with our brothers and sisters, when can we find time to blow upon the dying embers, to rekindle the flame that is our life and our hope? How can we make space for prayer during our working day? And if we by chance happen upon an unexpected interval, how can we expect to achieve sufficient stillness to pray before we are forced to return once more to our task?

The answer to the problem of praying in the market place is not to blame the events of our life because they distract us from our prayer, but to use them to feed it. Returning to the image of the dying embers, we can build a wind-break around them and then kneel down and blow upon the coals from time to time or, once the flames are well established, we can remove the protection and let the wind take over. If our fire is properly constructed it will not only withstand the bigger draught but burn with far greater intensity than if we had retained our protective barrier.

And so it can be with our prayer. Once we learn to feed it with the things around us and with the commonplace events of our day it will burn like a forest fire that no human power can extinguish.

In discussing how this may be done we must return to the basic premise about prayer, that it is an act of the will. If we wish to weave prayer into the fabric of our lives we must deliberately direct our most mundane thoughts and aspirations God-wards and make a lived reality of the intellectual conviction that God is ever with us. In the words of a familiar hymn we may pray:

> God be in my head,
> And in my understanding,
> God be in my eyes,
> And in my looking,
> God be in my mouth,
> And in my speaking,
> God be in my heart,
> And in my thinking,
> God be at my end,
> And at my departing.

This constant referring to God during the course of our day is known as the practice of the presence of God. It is, as we have said, an act of the will, and like all prayer it is begun as a deliberate manoeuvre and after a period of practice and fidelity can become second nature. Like an aeroplane we rev our engines and taxi down the runway, until one day we realize to our astonishment that we have been flying for some time without knowing it.

But let us begin at the beginning; let us see how one person's thoughts can be directed Godwards during an ordinary working day.

I wake in the morning (and though this is my day, 'I' could mean you, me, anyone) and my mind, still misted with sleep, moves upwards. It may be a silent 'glance', a surge of gratitude for a good sleep, for the early promise of a beautiful day or an ill-articulated groan for help to face what the morning may bring. Whatever the shape of our waking thoughts they can be directed Godwards. Then, in the quiet moments before I get up, I can pray with greater or lesser intensity. Perhaps I repeat the 'morning offering' of my childhood:

> My God, I offer you this day
> All I shall think or do or say ...

As I lie there quietly thinking of this and that, remembering the events of yesterday or anticipating those of today, I raise my mind in thanksgiving or in humble petition: Lord, let it be; let it not be.

I get up. The minutes spent in washing and dressing are all 'free time', time that can be used for prayer if I so choose. Ten minutes here, ten minutes there – these are the precious minutes that can be deliberately used to build the foundations of constant prayer. If the morning is my time for 'formal' prayer, I now compose myself to be still. I sit with a cup of tea trying to clear the fog of sleep from my mind. After a while I feel alert and ready to concentrate, or perhaps I feel sick with the special early morning nausea of those who haven't slept enough. No matter. This half hour is for God, for watching and waiting on his pleasure. What I feel matters not at all; the painful sweet longing for the Absolute or the humiliating longing only for my breakfast. This is his business not mine. The psalms I read may have as much impact as reading a telephone directory – or they

I go to my work and to a different mode of praying. Here my mind is fully engaged with the work in hand. I am a doctor and here in the hospital there are diagnoses to be made, problems to be solved, patients to be seen, relatives to be comforted, students to be taught. Here I sing no hymns, read no psalms, but work with and for my God. Christ's is the face I look for in the unconscious motorcyclist rushed in off the motorway, his help I invoke as I struggle to set up the blood transfusion, and it is he whom I thank when a brief flicker of an eyelid shows that consciousness is not far away and that this young man at least will be reprieved.

Of course, it doesn't always work this way, and it is only after I've been surly with a junior nurse or a neurotic patient that I remember that there went my God, disguised, in pain, and I knew him not. But, all in all, I do my best. I strive to be conscientious, to be patient with those who irritate me, to be loving to those who are afraid. A friend once gave me a holy card which said something like: 'What would Christ do in my position?' It is a sobering question to ask ourselves, especially in those moments when we are about to demand our rights, stand on our dignity or give someone a piece of our mind. It is a question that more often than not leads to a gentler course of action than we had planned, an acceptance of blame, an unsolicited attempt at reconciliation, and the results can be unexpected and very beautiful.

And so the day wears on. Perhaps I go to operate. The ten-minute silent scrubbing-up time is a bonus, as is the quarter of an hour that we have to wait for the anaesthetist to get the patient ready. This habit of praying while I am waiting for an operation to begin, or for a train, or for someone to come, has changed my life. Now, instead of getting irritated and impatient when I am kept waiting I relax and realize that I have been given an unexpected bonus, a gift of time to stoke my fire and warm myself beside it. When the waiting is over I am able to rise and smile, serene and grateful for God's free gift.

The day wears on again and I become tired and ill-tempered; I sit by the telephone and try fruitlessly to make contact with a colleague in another hospital. I seem thwarted at every turn: the line is engaged, then crossed, and then I am cut off. My exasperated 'God give me strength' is a cry from the depths.

At last it is time to go. I sit in my car and gaze at the line of cars ahead of me. No singing now. Wearily I raise my mind to God. There are no words, no thoughts, just an inclination of the soul at the close of a long day.

After supper I feel better and settle down with my family to watch television. The programme is not of my choice but it would be churlish to go, so I let my mind wander idly. Like everyone else my gaze is fixed on the screen, but I am focused beyond it. The figures come and go but I barely see them. My mind idles gently, thinking nothing in particular but perhaps repeating a snatch of a Psalm, perhaps not; it is simply focused on God.

At last it is bedtime. Half asleep, I strike a match

and light a candle. The flame flickers gently and I turn out the light. For ten minutes, perhaps twenty, I sit, looking at the dancing light. My mind is empty, dulled by fatigue but somehow peaceful and curiously 'open' to God. Sometimes it happens that I fall asleep as I pray, but weary and with all defences down I am just a child before my Father and I know that:

Nothing is so beautiful as a child who falls asleep while saying its prayers, God says.

Charles Péguy

Like all average days, this one that I have sketched does not exist. There are not many days when I pray from morning to night in this way. But the description is true for some part of each day, and this awareness of God comes and goes, so that there are days when I am always conscious of him and others when I pay him little heed.

The day I have described is, of course, my own, the life of a busy professional person whose time is taken up with a multitude of demands, both intellectual and emotional. The principle, however, of weaving prayer into the fabric of our working life is the same for all men and women. The pattern for each will naturally be different, but let us look briefly at the day of an average housewife. Let us call her Mary; she could be Margaret or Kate, Pat or Diana – Mrs Everyman.

Her waking will be shared; perhaps it will be to the joyous awareness of the physical and emotional warmth of the man who lies at her side. Her heart, filled with that special tenderness that we feel for those we love when they are asleep, may rise in an unspoken prayer of thanksgiving or intercession for her beloved. Or perhaps it will be a waking devoid of all tangible joy – the shrill of an alarm clock or the cry of a baby demanding to be fed. But however the day begins, in anguish or in deep joy, Mary can cry out to God in the early morning. It may be the few minutes she is alone waiting for the kettle to boil, a half hour feeding the baby, or merely snatched glances and cries for help as she searches for a clean shirt, a missing football boot or a vital exercise book that has been cleared away with yesterday's papers.

But when the door slams for the last time, or she returns from delivering the youngest child to school, there comes the possibility of 'wasting time' with her maker. It is at this point that the need for discipline and a re-thinking of priorities emerges. There is the house to be tidied, the dishes to be washed, and clothes to be laundered, for 'woman's work is never done'.

True, woman's work *is* never done, but it can be shifted about a little and spaces made for more important things. Does it really matter that the breakfast table is cleared at once, the living-room vacuumed, the beds made immediately? Perhaps ten minutes spent over a cup of coffee and twenty in quiet prayer could be fitted in on a regular basis in just the same way that she would make time to waste with a friend who called unexpectedly. As in so many things, it is a question of making the decision to do it, of starting today rather than next week, and of beginning again and again when one has failed.

Upon this foundation of formal prayer may be built the wondrous castle of continuous communication with God. The 'wasted' half hour of silent prayer will flow into the spaces of the day. The walk to the supermarket will become an extension of the quiet time, and the faces of the people in the street icons of the risen Christ. The more we seek God in prayer the more we shall be attuned to see him in the world around us, in the things of creation, in the things that man has made, and in man himself. But we must tune ourselves, hone our spirits, if we are to find heaven in a grain of sand, the mystery of the godhead in an electric sewing machine and the Christ in stranger's guise.

For the mother of the family, the woman of the house, it is in people that she will most often meet with Christ. There is an ancient Gaelic rune of hospitality:

> I saw a stranger yestreen:
> I put food in the eating place,
> Drink in the drinking place,
> Music in the listening place;
> And in the blessed name of the Triune
> He blessed myself and my house,
> My cattle and my dear ones.
> And the lark said in her song
>   Often, often, often,
> Goes the Christ in stranger's guise
>   Often, often, often,
> Goes the Christ in stranger's guise.

In stranger's guise indeed he comes; early in the
morning in dressing-gown and curlers, face stained
with tears and fingers with nicotine. Today's casual-
ties do not lie only in the ditch on the Jericho road,
waiting for us to stop or to pass by, but knock
importunately upon our doors, a request for a cup
of sugar thinly concealing the need for comfort and
someone to share the pain. Christopher Jones, an
American poet with an exceptionally acute vision
of Christ in his neighbour, writes:

> Do not be afraid to see
> What is really there.
> Do not be afraid of the next day,
> the next hour,
> the next moment.
> There He is.
> Do not be afraid of Him!
> He is a woman old and wrinkled
> and smelling like wine, and dirty
> with sneakers and a torn sweater and a handbag
> cracked and torn,
> Smoking a just-rolled cigarette.
> Do not be afraid of His language
> or the looks of Him
> or the smell of Him.
> He is your God.

From *Listen Pilgrim*

Perhaps the ability to see through the disguise, the
mask that conceals the suffering Christ, is partly a
cultural one. Those who work with the mentally
handicapped are in part naturally equipped and

in part trained to see the powerless, the scorned, the rejected Christ among those with whom they work. And yet they may be blind to the wretched, lonely, wounded heart so well disguised in the rich woman who cannot bring herself to kiss a dribbling mongol boy. And yet he is there, he comes disguised in all men, in the long-haired hippy strumming a guitar in the Underground no less than in the dedicated nurse's gentle ministrations. He calls out to us in different voices and in different places, for a smile at the cash desk in the supermarket, or for a patient ear in the train when we would rather read or pray.

And what of all the other workers, and those who have no work? Whatever the pattern of our day, tranquil or chaotic, we can pray if we choose. Those who work with their hands rather than with their heads are perhaps in a privileged position, for their minds are much freer to ponder on the mysteries of God and to pray. Gardening, farming, brick-laying, grave-digging, or crafts such as bookbinding, pottery, or printing, are often the chosen tasks of men and women who are intellectually equipped for work which is much more demanding. What a terrible 'waste' of talent goes on among the Little Brothers of Charles de Foucauld or in Cistercian monasteries, where men with university degrees spend their working day in factories, tilling the soil or looking after chickens. This is folly indeed in worldly terms, but our system of values is turned upside down by Christ, the folly of men becomes the wisdom of God.

The state of recollection by which communication with God is woven into our day depends very much upon fidelity to formal prayer. If we discipline ourselves to pray for half an hour each morning, or at some other time, to go each day to Mass, to read the Scriptures, then it is likely that awareness of God will never be far away, for we shall become alert to the 'spaces' in our day and automatically fill them with prayer. If, conversely, we are lazy about the deliberate 'wasting' of time with God, then it is not long before a mind busy with a million things loses its awareness of the transcendent and with it the gift of continual prayer. Recognition of God in the market place is always dependent upon getting to know him in the desert.

And as always, because we are at the same time created and supernatural beings, the life of the spirit is inextricably interwoven with the most mundane aspects of our humanity. I no longer worry whether my dryness in prayer is the result of indigestion and insomnia or the dark night of the soul. Does it matter? In the same way I cannot know whether my joy during the liturgy is a spiritual gift or simply the result of my being exhilarated by the music or the presence of a loved one. Again, does it matter? Is not the music God's gift? Is not love and friendship part of his revelation to me? As I relax into acceptance of my nature, part flesh, part spirit, I realize that there is no separating the human and the divine, that all is one and all is gift.

CHAPTER VIII

The Call of the Desert

I am going to lure her and lead her out into
the wilderness and speak to her heart.

Hosea 2 : 16

The gospels tell us on more than one occasion that
Jesus rose very early in the morning and went to a
place apart in order to pray. He went the day after
he had healed Simon Peter's mother-in-law and the
many other sick people who had come to the house
when the word got around that he was there; before
he chose the twelve apostles he spent the whole
night in prayer and, as the hour of his passion approached, he went to the Mount of Olives to sweat
out in prayer his fear and the final surrender to the
will of his Father.

If we are to take our discipleship seriously then
we must look at the way Jesus prayed, for he was 'a
man like us in all things but sin'. Jesus was a busy
man: he was a preacher, a healer, a man who in
three years gathered so many followers that the
authorities saw him as a threat to the security of
the State. If a revolutionary is a man who calls
upon others to change their whole way of thinking
and acting, then Jesus was a revolutionary. True, he
preached that those who live by the sword shall

perish by the sword, but his message was one of non-violent revolution. And, being a man 'like us' he was a family man with all the responsibilities and demands, the highs and the lows, the moments of grief and rejoicing that are part and parcel of our human condition. For most of his adult life he lived at home with his mother and in the three years of his active ministry we are told quite clearly that he had many deep personal relationships. A man living a life of freely chosen celibacy to the full, he supported and was supported by those he loved; by John and by Mary Magdalen, Peter, Lazarus, Mary and Martha.

So, by all our modern standards, Jesus was a busy man, stretched to the limit physically and emotionally by the demands of his work, by his family responsibilities and by the revolutionary fire, the zeal for his Father's house, that burned within him and led him to the Cross. But he prayed. Not just on Sundays, not just in the synagogue on the Sabbath, but from time to time he left the sick unhealed, the mourning uncomforted, the ignorant untaught, and stole off by himself or with a few close friends to spend time in prayer.

If Jesus was 'a man like us', are we not men and women like Jesus was? If he needed this time apart, do we not need it also? Perhaps it is not enough that we should worship as a community on a Sunday, that we should kneel at our beds each night. Perhaps, like Jesus, we must, from time to time, down tools and go off on our own in order to be alone with our God.

When we go to a place apart to 'make a retreat', to face ourselves and God in solitude, we are putting into practice the belief that prayer is the most important thing in our lives, witnessing our signature to the Credo that we recite each Sunday.

Making retreats is the penultimate in waste of time – with God. (The monastic and the eremitical life are the ultimate.) Actually to spend a day, three days, a week, away from our work and yet not on holiday is folly indeed – the folly of standing naked before the living God. Perhaps it is because it is so foolish in human terms that we need to distance ourselves from the rest of the world, that we need to go out into the desert.

The 'desert', of course, in this context, is a generic term for any place apart where we go to be alone with God. It may be an attic in our house, a nearby convent, a hotel room, a monastery or a deserted cottage on the moors. What matters is not where it is but that we go there alone, without radio, television, novels or a pile of unwritten letters. The provisions we carry will vary according to our personality and more particularly according to our experience in such expeditions. Fear of the unknown always makes the beginner travel heavy and, afraid of being driven desperate by boredom we pack our bags with books, Bibles and notebooks, some knitting, our sketching materials, golf clubs and so on. As in all travel, we learn by experience that it is much easier in the long run to travel light; but we must learn this ourselves. It is only after we have come back from our fifth or sixth retreat, with books unopened and paints untouched, that we shall gain the courage to go with just our Bible and our Wellington boots.

What happens to us on retreat depends upon all sorts of things and, of course, it depends entirely upon God. But given that grace 'co-operates' with nature and that God 'works' through ordinary events and people, the results of a retreat will be determined by our inner attitude towards it and by the external factors involved. (Perhaps it is as well to state here that I am deliberately using the word 'retreat' in a rather loose way, to cover anything from a week spent in a hermitage to a day of recollection at a nearby monastery.)

By far the most important factor is, of course, the attitude with which we approach the retreat. The more we strive to be open to what God is asking of us, the more we shall be disposed to 'hear' what he has to say.

Most retreats which are 'given' in retreat houses are structured around talks and periods of prayer and reading. This is good, for we all need new insights and inspiration in the matters of the spirit. But let us not deceive ourselves. The 'success' of our retreat will not depend upon the retreat-giver but upon us and upon the generosity and courage with which we lay ourselves open to God. If we spend one day or three days busily moving from conference to discussion group to liturgy and back again, we shall have had the equivalent of an express bus trip through the Sahara. We shall not have experienced the desolation and emptiness of spirit that comes from an appreciation of our own smallness and vulnerability in a harsh land. Periods of solitude with God are not called a 'desert experience' for nothing. Weary stumbling across miles of sand, hour after hour, towards a barely discerned oasis, is a frightening experience and so is going apart to be with God. Sudden sandstorms fill our eyes and mouths with sand, and we crouch desperately behind what little shelter we have, or move forward in pain and confusion; night falls and the heat of the sun gives way to a biting cold, for which we are absurdly unprepared. And so it can be in our spiritual desert. A remark by a retreat-giver, a phrase from the Scriptures or the generous facing of some long-ignored demand can lead to a lostness, a feeling of having been stripped naked, that makes us wonder at the folly of our having come at all. But if, as in the desert, we have come so far that there is no turning back, then we can only stumble onwards in faith, in the belief that somewhere, beyond the furthest dunes, lies the next oasis.

Of course this kind of confrontation experience that I have been hinting at is no everyday affair. It happens at times of crisis or decision making in our lives. But it is precisely because we deliberately fill our lives with distractions that it is often necessary to withdraw in order to face the issues involved. It is indeed a terrifying thing to fall or to throw ourselves into the hands of the living God, and those who have done it will know that the peace to be found in the desert is quite other than that described in the travel brochures.

Just as the physical desert varies, so will our experience of solitude. There will be early mornings spent watching sunrises that leave us speechless with wonder, and hours of slow, thirsty walking in which we know nothing but our human frailty and the loneliness of the terrain through which we walk. More often than not we shall be aware of nothing but our own emptiness, but experience will reveal that, in moments that we do not recognize, our leaky cisterns are patched and filled and we return to the market place somehow refreshed and renewed. We may put it down to the change of air, to the extra sleep or the brilliance of the retreat-giver – and of course God works through all of these things – but the fact is that if we re-arrange our lives, pack a bag, take a train and walk half a mile in order to meet our God then he will come more than part way to meet us. Are we not reminded that there is no father who would give his child a stone when he asks for bread?

But what does all this talk of sand and oases mean for ordinary people? Where is our nearest desert and how do we set about getting there? The first and most important step is the decision to go. It is the making of the act of faith that says this time 'wasted' with God is time well spent and that be we bishop, doctor, housewife or supermarket manager we are not indispensable. It is that basic turning upside down of priorities that leads us to say 'My strength comes from God and therefore if I am to be an apostle I must organize my life so that I have time to be with him alone'. Of course, this is easier said than done – but it can be done. A half day in a week can be found if we really put our minds to it. (How easily we forget the day or two that they managed without us last time we had 'flu or went to our grandmother's funeral!)

So – once we have made the decision, where should we go? While we are still new to this way of life it is helpful to go to retreat houses or monasteries where the life is organized so as to make conditions for prayer optimal. It can be a great help to go somewhere that is in very beautiful countryside, for it is somehow easier to be alone in the countryside than in a small room. It is not without reason that most monasteries are built in the country, for to walk among the hills or to sit on the edge of a lake has a quieting effect on the spirit that is hard to achieve in the centre of the town.

The availability of beautiful liturgy can be enormously helpful, especially for a person making a 'private' retreat. The hospitality offered by monastic houses is especially valuable in this respect, for attendance at the choral office can not only be helpful devotionally, but may transform loneliness into peaceful solitude. There is, too, a curiously powerful witness given by the very existence of monasteries. The sight of men and women, young and old, who have opted for what is, in human terms, a crassly foolish way of life quite simply because there is a God, can be both a disturbing and a strengthening experience. I don't think I shall ever forget the effect that attending a monastic funeral had upon me. The sight of a hundred men following the coffin of an old monk to his last resting place, and the knowledge that each of them, from the old scholar in his eighties to the eighteen-year-old novice, had vowed or would soon vow to live and die in this place, was an awe-inspiring experience.

When we have gained a little experience in 'wasting time' with God, in walking and sitting and doing nothing but waiting on his pleasure in a place designed for worship, we shall find that it is possible in many other places. But wherever we go it is helpful to go apart, to leave our world behind, even if it is only for a few hours, to go in search of solitude and of God. There are a number of reasons for this which are largely psychological but are in no way to be despised for this fact. The sheer physical cut-off from our own affairs makes recollection much easier, as does the serenity that comes from the knowledge that no one can ring us up or knock on our door.

It is, too, easier to be faithful to a decision to spend a half day in prayer if we have taken a bus and climbed halfway up a mountain to do so. The overpowering urge to go home and do something 'useful' is much easier to resist if one has distanced oneself from one's responsibilities. Where we go will depend upon our tastes and upon what is available; it may be that we can spend half a day a week at a nearby convent or monastery, or go for a weekend to someone's empty seaside cottage. What matters is not where we go, but that we should go, and go regularly, for, as in all prayer, discipline is vital.

If we do not make a positive decision and fix a date, then our diaries will become filled and the weeks slip by.

The frequency with which we go will depend in part upon the demands made upon us and in part upon our response to those demands. If we have no free time in the foreseeable future we should ask ourselves very seriously if we are not unwittingly overdrawing upon our emotional and spiritual reserves. In the end it is a matter of priorities, of having the faith to say 'It is more important that I spend this weekend in prayer than in attending that meeting', or, 'This afternoon I am going off to pray and I'll do the washing tomorrow'. It is a humiliating business to catch sight of oneself creating time to do something one wants to do, after having been quite certain that there was none available for less agreeable demands. As in all areas of the spiritual life, it is very easy to fool oneself.

And what do we do when we get there? Just how should we spend this three hours, this day or this week? After some experience it is possible to learn the art of being alone so as to be available to God. We may spend our time walking, sitting on a log or a hillside, gazing into the distance or twiddling a piece of dried grass in our fingers. We may read or we may sleep, we may garden, sew, knit, string beans: any quiet manual task that leaves our mind free to pray or just to free-wheel gently as the spirit moves. There is a balance that can be achieved between all these activities but in particular between formal prayer, spiritual reading and the sort of quiet work that leaves one's mind peacefully available for reflection and prayer. It is useful, in the beginning, to seek advice from someone experienced in this way of life and there is a curious freedom that comes from being given a plan to follow, of being set to do two hours' gardening and then an hour's reading or a half hour's prayer. With time, of course, we acquire self-knowledge and an understanding of our own individual requirements for solitude and tolerance of time alone. Then we can become 'self-winding' and take ourselves off for a day with nothing more than a packed lunch and a copy of the New Testament or the Psalms.

If the market place is where the people are, then the desert is where we go to be alone. We go, not to escape the demands of our lives but so that we may be renewed, refreshed and restored. We set out in faith, confident that if we go in search of God he will come to us and that this encounter, however we experience it, will give us strength. To take time off from our work to be alone with God is to admit our need for him, our dependence upon him and this indeed is the beginning of wisdom.

CHAPTER IX

The Word of God

> Your word is a lamp for my steps and a light for my path.
>
> Psalm 119: 105

The concept of the Word of God is a scriptural one and it embraces not only the written word, the Old and New Testaments, but the whole mystery of Christ alive and with us today. That there is a close relationship between our hearing of the Word and our prayer is something that we learn by experience. The relationship is a multi-faceted one, for our reading and hearing of the scriptures 'feeds' our prayer, and our prayer sends us back to the Word as our hunger for God grows.

It is one of the great mysteries of the spiritual life that we do not always 'hear' the Word when it is spoken. It is not just a matter of good intention but a curious mixture of factors, psychological and spiritual. Those who live in monasteries and are exposed daily to the reading of the Scriptures are familiar with the feeling of humiliation that besets those who waken with a start to the familiar phrase 'This is the Word of the Lord', and realize that they quite simply have been thinking about something else and have no idea what the reading was about.

Much, too, depends upon the way the Scriptures are read and it is a quite different experience to hear a passage, for example from the book of Job, read too rapidly or over dramatically, and read slowly and lovingly by someone who treasures what he reads. But there is more to hearing the Word than these rather mundane observations. The more we pray, the greater is our hunger for God and the greater our openness to his Word. There is a curious and marvellous phenomenon of heightened receptivity to the Scriptures that is God's gift to those who are faithful in prayer. Passages heard many times before suddenly strike home with a new power and become in truth God's personal communication to us. A phrase or a command heard often before, and that had always seemed meant for someone else, will one day come with the urgency of a telegram and the name on the envelope is no longer 'Everyman' but 'You'. The familiar story of Christ's conversation with the rich young man in Luke 18: 18 is just such a passage:

> If you would be perfect, go sell what you have and give it to the poor and come follow me.
>
> Luke 18: 18

St Antony, a rich young Egyptian living in the third century, was suddenly hit by hearing this passage read in church. He left all he had to follow a call that he knew was addressed directly to him and in so doing became the father of Christian Monasticism. Nearly a century later, the young Augustine of Hippo read of Antony's conversion and realized that these words, too, were for him. Augustine writes of his conversion:

I probed the hidden depths of my soul and wrung its pitiful secrets from it, and when I mustered them all before the eyes of my heart, a great storm broke within me, bringing with it a great deluge of tears ... For I felt that I was still the captive of my sins, and in my misery kept crying 'How long shall I go on saying "tomorrow, tomorrow"? Why not now? Why not make an end of my ugly sins at this moment?'

I was asking myself these questions, weeping all the while with the most bitter sorrow in my heart, when all at once I heard the sing-song voice of a child in a nearby house. Whether it was the voice of a boy or girl I cannot say, but again and again it repeated the refrain: 'Take it and read, take it and read'. At this time I looked up, thinking hard whether there was any kind of game in which children used to chant words like these, but I could not remember ever hearing them before. I stemmed my flood of tears and stood up, telling myself that this could only be a divine command to open my book of Scripture and read the first passage on which my eyes should fall. For I had heard the story of Antony and I remembered how he had happened to go into a church while the Gospel was being read and had taken it as a counsel addressed to himself when he heard the words 'Go home and sell all that belongs to you.

Give it to the poor, and so the treasure you have shall be in heaven; then come back and follow me.' (Matthew 19: 21) By this divine pronouncement he had been converted to you.

So I hurried back to the place where Alypius was sitting, for when I stood up to move away I had put down the book containing Paul's Epistles. I seized it and opened it, and in silence I read the first passage on which my eyes fell: 'Not in revelling and drunkenness, not in lust and wantonness, not in quarrels and rivalries. Rather arm yourselves with the Lord Jesus Christ; spend no more thought on nature and nature's appetites.' (Romans 13: 13) I had no wish to read more and no need to do so. For in an instant, as I came to the end of the sentence, it was as though the light of confidence flooded into my heart and all the darkness of doubt was dispelled.

Confessions of St Augustine, Book VIII
Chapter 12

Augustine lived in the fourth century and became, after his conversion, one of the great doctors of the Church and an indefatigable proclaimer of the Word of God, that Word of which it is said in the letter to the Hebrews:

The word of God is something alive and active: it cuts like any double-edged sword but more finely: it can slip through the place where the soul is divided from the spirit, or the joints from the marrow; it can judge the secret emotions and thoughts.

Hebrews 4: 12

It is not just the demands of the Scriptures that batter us until we capitulate, but a growing sense of wonder at the truth of it all. Different passages will strike us at different times, according to our 'condition' of soul and spirit. One day we shall be filled with an agonizing realization at the truth of Christ's statement that he who would follow must take up his cross each day, and that the grain of wheat must fall to the ground and die before it can bear fruit. As we do battle in our souls with some apparently unreasonable demand of God, we both weep at the unfairness of it and at the same time gain strength from the 'certainty born of faith' that out of this pruning there will certainly come new growth.

Then, there will be moments of unexpected joy when we shall want to leap up and say: 'It's true! It's true!' because we realize the truth of some statement such as Paul's remark that neither hunger, nakedness, persecution nor the sword can separate us from God's love. (I remember just such a moment when I was in prison and caused considerable confusion among the prison authorities by saying to the British Consul that he must tell my family that Romans 8 was true!) This experience becomes commonplace and registers in a lower but none the less marvellous key as we become familiar with the psalms.

The law of the Lord is perfect,
it revives the soul.
The rule of the Lord is to be trusted,
it gives wisdom to the simple.

The precepts of the Lord are right,
they gladden the heart.
The command of the Lord is clear,
it gives light before the eyes.

The fear of the Lord is holy,
abiding for ever.
The decrees of the Lord are truth
and all of them just.

They are more to be desired than gold,
than the purest of gold,
and sweeter are they than honey,
than honey from the comb.

Psalm 19

This growing familiarity with the psalms and the Scriptures leads to a curious and wonderful process by which a man becomes slowly impregnated with the Word of God. We see this phenomenon at its height in the writings of the Fathers of the Church and some of the monastic writers who have so absorbed the Word that passages of Scripture are no longer deliberately quoted but flow quite naturally from their pens and are inextricably interwoven with their reflections. Such a process of assimilation of the Word of God is to be found in the writings of

St Anselm, a Benedictine monk who was Abbot of Bec in Normandy and became Archbishop of Canterbury in 1093. In the following selection from Anselm's 'Prayer to Christ' we see how fragments from different Psalms and the Scriptures have become his own prayer:

What shall I say? What shall I do? Whither shall I go?
Where shall I seek him? Where and when shall I find him?
Whom shall I ask? Who will tell me of my beloved? 'for I am sick from love'.
'The joy of my heart fails me';
my laughter 'is turned into mourning';
 'my heart and my flesh fail me';
'but God is the strength of my heart, my portion for ever'.
'My soul refuses comfort', unless from you, my dear.
 'Whom have I in heaven but you,
and what do I desire on earth but you?'
I want you, I hope for you, I seek you;
'to you my heart has said, seek my face';
'your face, Lord, have I sought;
 turn not your face from me'.
 From *The Meditations and Prayers of St Anselm*

This process of assimilation cannot leave a man unchanged, and we see especially in the Old Testament prophets men who have become totally taken over by the word of God. The prophet Jeremiah describes his battle with the Lord:

The word of Yahweh has meant for me
insult, derision, all day long.
I used to say 'I will not think about him,
  I will not speak in his name any more'.
Then there seemed a fire burning in my heart,
imprisoned in my bones.
The effort to restrain it wearied me,
I could not bear it.

Jeremiah 20 : 8

The prophets, driven by the fire that burns within them, are forced, often unwillingly, to wield this two-edged sword that pierces men in the secret places of their hearts. Their words are seldom welcomed, their way is hard and lonely and often leads to the cross. It is small wonder that the way of the prophet has ever been a calling and not a profession; the prophet is the father and mother of the wild word of God:

> My word is your child.
> To mother it, gentle or wild,
> I chose you.

Peter De Rosa

This 'mothering' of the word of God is especially the task of those who are called to preach the Gospel but, in an increasingly secular world, it is often lay men and women who find themselves compelled to 'stand up and be counted' or to speak out against corruption and injustice. God chooses whom he pleases to declare his word, both the gentle word of love and compassion and the wild word of truth and justice.

But the word of God is not just for churchmen and those who work for justice, it is for all of us, and if we are serious in our quest for the transcendent, we must become familiar with the Scriptures. Once again it is a question of discipline, of doing battle with that curious spiritual inertia that the Latin American theologian Juan Luis Segundo calls 'the law of minimum effort' and St Paul speaks of as 'the flesh'. Just as we must find time each day to pray, so we must find time too, to read the Bible. If we are to open our hearts to the Scriptures, to absorb the word of God, we must read as our forefathers did, slowly and meditatively, pondering the words in our heart. This is what is known in the monastic tradition as '*Lectio Divina*' and it is quite different from reading a novel or from studying, for it is a process whereby after only a few phrases reading may flow into prayer and back again.

Just as in *Lectio Divina* we must learn to read attentively, so we must learn to listen when the word is read to us in church. It is only if we make a deliberate effort to listen that we shall begin to hear the word which has the power to change our lives. Familiarity with a particular piece of Scripture can make a great difference to our ability to understand the meaning of what is read to us, and a few minutes spent before Mass 'preparing' the readings of the day can make all the difference to our 'hearing' the Word or allowing it to pass once more over our heads.

There are many different approaches that we must make to the word if we are even to begin to understand the richness of our Christian heritage. Slow, meditative reading is one avenue, attentive listening to the spoken word another. The formal study of the Scriptures is another 'way in' which will open up to us whole new vistas of the meaning of Christianity. For the theologically unlettered there is so much of the Bible that is obscure, and it is only when we begin to appreciate its historical and cultural background that we can take a step forward from the fundamentalist approach of our childhood to an adult appreciation. It is here that an elementary theology course or Bible study group can be of great help in opening up for us this priceless gift, the revelation of God himself.

Over twenty years ago, when I was a first year medical student, a priest friend gave me a battered little book of selected daily Scripture readings. A week or so later he wrote, and I still have the letter, 'But I forgot to tell you what to look for in the gospels. A person. Just that. And then you will be finding him everywhere, even in the extraordinary works he puts inside a dogfish to make it go.' I treasured the letter because I loved him, but it was many years before I even began to understand what he meant as the little brown book somehow got laid on one side and I never got round to reading it.

What he was talking about, of course, was the word of God – but what the theologians now write with a capital letter: Word. Here we must distinguish between the Scriptures as the inspired message of God to his people and between his final and ultimate self-communication; the sending of his son, Jesus Christ, the Word of God. At first meeting this concept of the 'word of God', writ sometimes small and sometimes big, can be not only confusing but irritating. Our minds, used to clear-cut definitions, cannot cope with such apparently woolly thinking, with ideas and images that flow one into the other. Once, however, we accept that we are human beings struggling to articulate, to communicate a truth only part-understood, a message only partly received, then we can begin to understand that our very ignorance is the beginning of wisdom.

St John begins his gospel:

> In the beginning was the Word:
> the Word was with God
> and the Word was God.
>
> John 1 : 1

He goes on to tell us that:

> The Word was made flesh,
> he dwelt amongst us.
>
> John 1 : 14

It is the Word of God made flesh that we meet, not only in the person of Jesus, the man of strength and compassion, of fiery integrity and joyous humanity upon whom we may dare to model ourselves, but in the risen Christ who lives in Paul and the other disciples. Once we grasp the idea that Christ lives on in us we start to recognize him not only in the saints who have gone before us but in the people among whom we live. We begin to understand the mystery of the living Word of the Father who, dwelling in man, pitches his tent among us and fulfils his promise that he will be with us to the end of the world.

This meeting with the Word of God is the climax of anyone's life. He may come to us in a sudden moment of recognition as he did to Mary Magdalen on Easter morning, or to the disciples on the road to Emmaus, or with the wind and fire of a pente-costal event. We may discern his presence in our lives through an intellectual process or through our hearts, in a cataclysmic moment of awakening or through a slow process of dawning understanding. However we meet him, when we do, we shall find ourselves afraid to meet his gaze and yet unable to go on as if nothing had happened. Then indeed we shall begin to meet him everywhere – in mountains and sunsets, in floods and earthquakes, in priests and in prostitutes, and 'even in the extraordinary works he puts inside a dogfish to make it go'.

CHAPTER X

Praying the Psalms

If any be afflicted, let him pray, and if any be
merry let him sing psalms.

James 5: 13

It is with some diffidence that I embark upon this
chapter because my experience of praying the
psalms is limited to a few years. I attempt it, however, in an effort to share a discovery which has
added a new dimension to my life of prayer.

Joseph Gelineau, who translated the psalms from
the original Hebrew into French, thus regaining
much of their imagery and poetry, describes them
as religious songs, but more powerfully as 'a series
of shouts: shouts of love and hatred; shouts of
suffering or rejoicing; shouts of faith or hope' (J.
Gelineau; *The Psalms*, Collins and Fount Paperbacks). They are the songs, the shouts, the poems
of people in all moods, and as such they cover the
whole range of human emotions and aspirations.
There is no mood of gratitude, joy, rage, vengeance
or terror that has not been expressed as a poem-
prayer of the Jewish people; and as familiarity with
them grows, we find that they speak not only for
the Jews who wrote them but for us and for all the
people of God. The psalms are the prayer of the

mystical body of Christ *par excellence*, because when we pray them we are crying out not only in our own name but in the name of all men.

Before going any further it seems important to say that the psalms are not easy to appreciate and they do not always have an immediate appeal. Although I have struggled on and off to use the psalms since I was a child at school, I have come to appreciate them only in the last few years, and in particular since I have participated in their public recitation. Even now, I find it much easier to pray them aloud with other people than on my own. Perhaps this is because poetry is written to be spoken and has its greatest impact in this way.

Another factor which has become important for me is familiarity. In a monastery one recites most of the one hundred and fifty psalms of the psalter each week; and although there are few that I know by heart, they have the familiarity of well-trodden paths, of a well-loved way; and, as with a person one knows well, or a familiar landscape, there is always something new to be found. Sometimes the emotion expressed strikes a chord with one's own feelings, so that, like someone playing a fruit machine in a desultory way, the images unexpectedly coincide and one is hit by a shower of coins.

The wealth of the psalms, like that of all prayer, is multi-faceted, both in its content and subjective effect. While theologians agree about most of the basic truths expressed in the psalms, those who pray them daily will often argue heatedly over what the psalms mean to them personally. For Roman Cath-

olics the change from the use of Latin to the
vernacular has highlighted one of the major differences in the way in which the psalms can be prayed.
Sung in Latin that one does not understand, the
Psalms can be frustratingly meaningless, or they can
be the most glorious wave of prayer that carries one
rather in the way that a swimmer is carried by the
tide. The recitation of the words and the beauty of
the music become a means of stilling the intellect to
leave the heart free for silent communication with
God. The same process occurs in many people even
when they understand the words that they are
singing, for they may become absorbed in a type of
prayer in which the words are no more than background music.

This pattern of praying the psalms is one which
is common to many people and I stress it because it
was some time before I learned not to feel guilty
about totally missing the meaning of a psalm that I
had read or sung. The other side to this way of
praying is the fact that the psalms are not only cries
from an anguished or joyous heart but are also
filled with the truths of our faith in God. Gelineau
writes: 'The psalms repeat in lyrical form the
teaching of the prophets; they recall the great events
of history (that of the people of Israel) that was itself
a divine revelation; they meditate on the covenant.'
Not only do the psalms tell the story of the people
of Israel, but they repeat again and again, with the
unself-conscious wonder of the poet and the child,
the basic tenets of our belief: that God made us,
that he loves us and that our only resting place is to

be found in him. With that acute perception of God in his creation that is his free gift to some, they remind us that our creator holds us all in the hollow of his hand:

How many are your works, O Lord!
In wisdom you have made them all.
The earth is full of your riches.
There is the sea, vast and wide,
with its moving swarms past counting,
living things great and small.
The ships are moving there
and the monsters you made to play with.

All of these look to you
to give them their food in due season.
You give it, they gather it up:
you open your hand, they have their fill.
You hide your face, they are dismayed;
you take back your spirit, they die,
returning to the dust from which they came.
You send forth your spirit, they are created
and you renew the face of the earth.

From Psalm 104

These words may seem at first sight simply naïve and beautiful poetry, yet they contain a depth of understanding that is often denied to the learned. The enchanting phrase 'the monsters you made to play with' expresses one of the most profound of theological truths: that creation is born of the joy of God, out of his love and laughter. We would do well to ponder on the mystery of the intelligence of the dolphin, an animal that not only communicates but has a sense of humour – surely a monster made to play with! Yet not only dolphins and whales, field mice and beetles, but man himself depends totally upon the continuous gift of life of the creator. When the rains come and the sun shines and the earth remains still, we lose sight of our dependence upon God; but occasionally there comes a year when the rains fail and the parched ground is strewn with the corpses of men and beasts:

> You hide your face, they are dismayed;
> you take back your spirit, they die,
> returning to the dust from which they came.

This understanding of the dependence of life upon God in no way conflicts with our increased scientific knowledge. My own experience of working in clinical medicine has greatly heightened my sense of mystery at the ways of God. The various 'coincidences', flashes of inspiration, that lead to scientific discovery I see as pure gift, and attendance at innumerable death-beds, where the combined expertise of doctors and nurses and modern technology has failed to save life, is summed up again by these words of the psalmist: 'You take back your spirit, they die'.

A constant theme in many of the psalms is the manner in which man should conduct his affairs in order to be worthy of the vision of God. Psalm 119 is just such a meditation:

'How shall the young remain sinless?' the psalmist enquires, and immediately there comes the reply:

By obeying your word.

Here the word of God is his law, his precepts, the instructions to his children and the writer prays:

Open my eyes that I may consider the wonders of your law (v. 18)

and

Make me grasp the ways of your precepts and I will muse on your wonders. (v. 27)

Verses 30–32 reveal a development in both the faith and the understanding of the writer, for he pledges himself to obey the decrees of the Lord whilst in the same breath begging for God to match his own fidelity:

I have chosen the way of truth
with your decrees before me.
I bind myself to do your will;
Lord, do not disappoint me.
(vv. 30–31)

The last line of this stanza is for me one of the most profound and beautiful in the psalter, for it

expresses the truth that obedience to the word of
God is the key to freedom of spirit:

> I will run the way of your commands;
> you give freedom to my heart. (v.32)

The same thoughts are repeated every few stanzas of
this long psalm, and yet their repetition is never
boring for it has the rhythm of gently lapping waves
and is the reiteration of a truth that can never be
told too often. Did lover ever ask the beloved to
cease saying 'I love you'? No – repetition here is
a process of reinforcing, of expressing love and
truth. This psalm is indeed a litany of love and
praise:

> The law from your mouth means more to me
> than silver and gold.   (v. 72)

He moves from this statement of the worth of the
law to a simple exclamation of delight:

> Lord, how I love your law!
> It is ever in my mind. (v. 97)

and gives yet another pledge of his fidelity:

> Your will is my heritage for ever,
> the joy of my heart.   (v. 97)

Much of the thought of this psalm is echoed in
Psalm 19:

The law of the Lord is perfect,
it revives the soul.
The rule of the Lord is to be trusted,
it gives wisdom to the simple.

The precepts of the Lord are right,
they gladden the heart.
The command of the Lord is clear,
it gives light to the eyes.

The fear of the Lord is holy,
abiding for ever.
The decrees of the Lord are truth
and all of them just.

They are more to be desired than gold,
than the purest of gold
and sweeter are they than honey,
than honey from the comb.

So in them your servant finds instruction;
great reward is in their keeping.

Another familiar theme in the psalter is the gratuitous nature of all things and the futility of man's
actions unless he is rooted in God:

If the Lord does not build the house,
in vain do its builders labour;
if the Lord does not watch over the city,
in vain does the watchman keep vigil.

In vain is your earlier rising,
your going later to rest,
you who toil for the bread you eat:
when he pours gifts on his beloved while
    they slumber.

From Psalm 127

Perhaps the psalms which arouse the most heated
emotions are the psalms of persecution. They range
from the anguished cry of the man in distress, with
which most people can identify, to cries for vengeance and violence that many people find frankly
disturbing. Many of those of the first variety are
very beautiful in their imagery and particularly
comforting to pray, for most of us are at our least
articulate when we are distressed. Psalm 102 is
especially poignant.

O Lord, listen to my prayer
and let my cry for help reach you.
Do not hide your face from me
in the day of my distress.
Turn your ear towards me
and answer me quickly when I call.

For my days are vanishing like smoke,
my bones burn away like a fire.
My heart is withered like the grass.
I forget to eat my bread.
I cry with all my strength
and my skin clings to my bones.

I have become like a pelican in the wilderness,
like an owl in desolate places.
I lie awake and I moan
like some lonely bird on a roof.
All day long my foes revile me;
those who hate me use my name as a curse.

The bread I eat is ashes;
my drink is mingled with tears.
In your anger, Lord, and your fury
you have lifted me up and thrown me down.
My days are like a passing shadow
and I wither away like the grass.

Psalm 88, too, is the prayer of a man in total desolation of spirit, who feels that he has been abandoned by God:

Let my prayer come into your presence.
O turn your ear to my cry.

For my soul is filled with evils;
my life is on the brink of the grave.
I am reckoned as one in the tomb:
I have reached the end of my strength.

The last two lines voice the extent of his loneliness:

Friend and neighbour you have taken away:
my one companion is darkness.

'My one companion is darkness' – how well this voices the cry of the incurably ill, the depressed and

those in prison. Perhaps one needs to have lived
through an experience of inescapable anguish to
grasp the full meaning of these words, but there
must be few adults in whom they do not strike a
chord.

Harder to understand and accept and, for many
people, impossible to pray, are the psalms which
cry to God to punish their oppressors. An example
is Psalm 94:

O Lord, avenging God,
avenging God, appear!
Judge of the earth, arise,
give the proud what they deserve!

How long, O Lord, shall the wicked,
how long shall the wicked triumph?
They bluster with arrogant speech;
the evil-doers boast to each other.

They crush your people, Lord,
they afflict the ones you have chosen.
They kill the widow and the stranger
and murder the fatherless child.

And they say: 'The Lord does not see;
the God of Jacob pays no heed.'
Mark this, most senseless of people;
fools, when will you understand?

Can he who made the ear, not hear?
Can he who formed the eye, not see?

Will he who trains nations, not punish?
Will he who teaches men, not have knowledge?

The power of the psalms of persecution first came home to me when I was in Chile, for it is in such totalitarian states that not only are people crushed, widows, strangers and orphans killed, but their murderers parade in public. Never will I forget the state funeral and pantomime of grief that was performed by men in high office for a colleague killed in an 'accident' which was believed by many to be an assassination. This rage and impotence is a deep human emotion and we do grave injustice to close our eyes to these sins that 'cry to heaven for vengeance'.

Even more difficult to accept as Christian prayer are the cries to the Lord to wreak violence upon oppressors; Psalm 109 is an example of such a prayer:

Appoint a wicked man as his judge;
let an accuser stand at his right.
When he is judged let him come out
    condemned;
let his prayer be considered as sin.

Let the days of his life be few;
let another man take his office.
Let his children become fatherless orphans
and his wife become a widow.

Let his children be wanderers and beggars
driven from the ruins of their home.

Let the creditor seize all his goods;
let strangers take the fruit of his work.

Let none show him any mercy
nor pity his fatherless children.
Let all his sons be destroyed
and with them their name be blotted out.

The key to the understanding of this psalm lies in
verses 16–17:

For he did not think of showing mercy
but persuaded the poor and the needy,
hounding the wretched to death.
He loved cursing; let curses fall on him.
He scorned blessing; let blessing pass him by.

The psalmist, then, is not calling down a curse
upon the helpless and the innocent, but is asking
that his oppressors should be treated as they have
treated him. It is the reverse of the old saying 'Do
as you would be done by' – the oppressed man asks
that those who persecute him should receive the
same treatment that they have meted out to him.
The first thing to understand in these psalms is
that they are the natural human response of those
who have been grievously wronged. There is no
denying that the sentiments expressed are not those
of Christ, who told us to turn the other cheek –
but that is indeed a hard saying, a counsel of per-
fection, and the power to forgive our enemies is a
grace, pure gift from God. If the oppressed in these
psalms have not been granted this very special grace

then let us not be so presumptuous as to judge them – for we cannot know how we would react if forced to see our children starve or our loved ones tortured and killed.

Understanding the mood of the psalmist in these violent prayers is one thing – to make his words our own is another. The difficulty experienced by many people is so great that the most violent verses are often omitted from community worship. For me the key to acceptance of these prayers lies in the Pauline concept of the Mystical Body of Christ – that we are all members of one body, and when one member is hurt the others cry out in pain with and for him. When, therefore, we pray these psalms, we are praying not about our own pain but crying out for the persecuted. We are articulating, not our own feelings but the feelings of the oppressed. We must leave it to God to judge those of his children who respond to injustice by wishing retribution on his persecutors.

This brings us to the idea that the words of what we pray have a very limited importance; it is what we intend in our 'hearts' (the heart in the Biblical sense means the will) that matters. There will be times when the words we pray will express the sentiments of our hearts – when we pray in our own words or in the words of a prayer that we have chosen. When we pray as a community rather than as an individual there will always be moments of dichotomy between the words we recite and what we feel. Much of this gulf has to do with our cultural background and our understanding of the symbolism used in the prayers chosen. Language which is intensely meaningful to one person may be meaningless or actually distasteful to another. I was faced with an instance of this not long ago when I listened to a sermon in which the priest spoke of 'hiding in the wounds of Christ'. This is a familiar concept to many Catholics but one which I have always found quite meaningless and frankly sentimental. I discussed my reaction with an experienced religious nun and came to understand that, because of my medical background, the symbolism of the wounds of Christ is quite different for me than for many other Christians. If I think of the wounds of Christ I see only the gaping, bleeding breaches in the skin which are a familiar part of my everyday work. The idea of someone hiding in a wound is unthinkable. I asked the sister to tell me what *she* understood by hiding in the wounds of Christ, and she asked me if I knew what it felt like to be protected by someone I loved – to be supported by the knowledge of his love for me. Now this was something that I experience and is immensely meaningful to me, so I found that the emotion we shared was similar – the sense of being protected by the love of God – it was just that the language, the symbolism used was different.

This difficulty about language in prayer is a frequent one, and if we are to pray in common as a community we must accept the fact that we shall often have to sing or recite words that do not have a lot of meaning for us. This difficulty may be overcome by understanding the problem and praying as it were behind the words, by using them as a vehicle for the prayer of our heart. If, then, we are asked to recite a prayer such as Psalm 108 let us listen to the words so that we may have some understanding of the depths of anguish of our brothers and at the same time pray in our hearts for what they do not have the strength to ask, the forgiveness of their persecutors. If we are able to pray in this way we shall grow in knowledge of our brotherhood with the oppressed: of our membership of the crucified mystical body of the Lord.

Praying the psalms should not only increase our awareness of the agony of the persecuted but instil in us a deep understanding of how we must live if we are to please God. The psalms echo the teaching found throughout the Old Testament, that the man who is pleasing to God is not merely the one who offers sacrifices but the one who is just and merciful, who protects the poor and the oppressed. Psalm 15 both asks and answers the question of who shall find favour with God:

> Lord, who shall be admitted to your tent
> and dwell on your holy mountain?
> He who walks without fault;
> he who acts with justice
> and speaks the truth from his heart;
> he who does not slander with his tongue;
> he who does no wrong to his brother,
> who casts no slur on his neighbour,
> who holds the godless in disdain,
> but honours those who fear the Lord;

he who keeps his pledge, come what may;
who takes no interest on a loan
and accepts no bribes against the innocent.
Such a man will stand firm for ever.

A different approach to the problem of what pleases
God is to be found in Psalm 73 where the psalmist
puzzles over the eternal paradox of the apparent
prosperity of the evil-doer:

For them there are no pains;
their bodies are sound and sleek.
They have no share in men's sorrows;
they are not stricken like others.

So they wear their pride like a necklace,
they clothe themselves with violence.
Their hearts overflow with malice,
their minds seethe with plots.

He comes at first to the very human conclusion that
his own life of virtue is a waste of time:

How useless to keep my heart pure
and wash my hands in innocence,
when I was stricken all day long,
suffered punishment day after day.

Then, after pondering the problem 'too hard for
my mind to understand' he is given the vision to
see the prosperity of the wicked in its true light,
that their glory is an ephemeral thing and their

evil brings about their downfall:

> I pierced the mysteries of God
> and understood what becomes of the wicked.
>
> How slippery the paths on which you set them;
> you make them slide to destruction.
> How suddenly they come to their ruin,
> wiped out, destroyed by terrors.

Psalms 73 finishes on a lyrical note, of mystical joy in the love of God, a theme repeated in many of the psalms.

> What else have I in heaven but you?
> Apart from you I want nothing on earth.
> My body and my heart faint for joy;
> God is my possession for ever.

Psalm 63 is perhaps the most powerful expression of this mystical longing for God alone. The psalmist uses the imagery of the desert to convey the extent of his desire:

> O God, you are my God, for you I long;
> for you my soul is thirsting.
> My body pines for you
> like a dry, weary land without water.

From the heights of joy to the depths of despair, from cries for vengeance to mystical prayer, the psalms embrace the whole gamut of man's relationship with God. Their poetry has a power of expression which transcends the barriers of our tongue-tied aspirations, and if we become familiar with them we shall grow in understanding not only of the ways of men but of those of God himself.

CHAPTER XI

Problems in Prayer

One must accept joyfully and with the whole will exactly the state of prayer which God makes possible for us here and now; we will have that and no other.'

Abbot John Chapman, *Spiritual Letters*

Problems in prayer, like all the problems in life, are much easier to cope with when we realize that they are shared by other people. If we do not articulate our difficulties in relationships with friends, family, children, and with God, we shall never reach that wonderful point where we can laugh at ourselves and admit that our difficulties are simply part of the condition of being human. It is amazing how a deep sense of guilt and inadequacy can vanish when we find that a problem we had thought was uniquely our own is shared by another. This discovery of the universal nature of difficulties in the spiritual life is a continuous one and is for me a constant source of encouragement and support. It is in this respect that honest discussion is so valuable, especially between those with many years of experience in prayer and those who are beginning. An example of this is the encouragement I received on finding that the difficulty I experience in disciplining myself in the matter of daily spiritual reading is shared by the very man who speaks to me of its importance. For a long time I thought he had it all under control and never faltered in his fidelity; but I discovered recently that he too finds such discipline is difficult to maintain and has to make frequent new beginnings. In the words of a popular song of some years ago:

> The world is full of famous men
> Who had to fall to rise again
> So pick yourself up, dust yourself down
> And start all over again!

Perhaps the greatest difficulty in prayer is the problem of fidelity, of keeping on keeping on. This problem is central in the spiritual life, not only in the sense that it is almost universal but in that from infidelity flow many of the other difficulties in prayer. There is an old and very profound truth that we do well to keep in mind: the more we pray the more we shall want to pray and, conversely, the less we pray the less we shall want or feel the need to pray.

Lack of fidelity to prayer stems partly from the lack of discipline but mainly from the fact that prayer is more often than not a dry and boring affair. If we embark upon our prayer expecting instant 'feed back' in terms of consolation and obvious answers to prayers of petition, then we shall be sadly disappointed. In reading the lives of the saints we learn that although feelings of sweetness and the love of God come to those who pray in earnest, they often disappear for long periods, sometimes years at a time, so that prayer must be continued in dryness and faith.

How ever, then, do people persevere in prayer? As in all things, fidelity to prayer is a grace, the free gift of God. The interaction between grace and nature is a problem over which theologians argue and which we can never fully understand. What we must strive to grasp, however, is the interplay between grace and faith. Grace is pure gift of God and we are free to respond to it or not; if we respond then our faith is deepened, we begin to appreciate the way God reveals himself to us in the Scriptures, in history, in the world around us and in our own lives. With this apprehension of the revelation of God our faith and hope increase and the natural response to this is a change of heart, a deepening of our Christian commitment. With an increase in faith in God comes an increase in love, a heightened longing for him and hence a determination to pray. Although, as time passes, the emotional satisfaction derived from prayer generally diminishes or disappears there is a concomitant deepening of faith which sustains us in increasing dryness.

What is exactly meant by 'dryness' in prayer? The term is frequently used but rarely explained. It is, quite simply, the absence of emotional satisfaction in prayer, the 'disappearance' of God. A person who has experienced great joy in prayer and a sense of loving God and of basking in his love may suddenly find that her prayer is distracted, that she no longer 'feels' any love for God and gets no satisfaction from prayer. This can be both confusing and distressing, for our natural reaction is to wonder what we are doing wrong, whether we have offended God that he has so palpably withdrawn his favour from us.

When this happens to someone who has been faithful to prayer and is striving to lead a life of Christian love, it is wise to take counsel with a priest experienced in prayer, for encouragement and advice may be needed if the person concerned is not to lose heart. Such counsel, of course, is not always available, so that we must learn a sort of on-the-spot examination for ourselves. If prayer which has been relatively sweet and easy suddenly becomes dry and difficult it is worth asking ourselves a few simple questions and examining our life style. It may be that we have ceased to be faithful to spiritual reading or that our lives have become too full of activity so that it is increasingly difficult to 'centre down' to pray. There may be, of course, a barrier between us and God which is caused by a deliberate failure to do what we know is his will for us.

The problem is such a personal one, however, that I hesitate to do more than mention the above difficulties. An approach that many people find helpful is a brief withdrawal, or retreat, to consider their situation and reorganize their lives. Even a couple of days away from our own work and home situation may be enough for us to discover that we have filled our lives so full of activity that we have unwittingly pushed God out to the periphery. This squeezing out of prayer time by over-activity is a constant problem for people who lead highly apostolic lives and become involved with more and more meetings, discussions and so on. It is all too easy to become so preoccupied with the greatness of the harvest and the scarcity of labourers that one forgets to give time to the Lord of the harvest. There is a very real sense in which the poor are always with us and our work is never done, so that if we do not make a conscious decision to 'waste time' with God, then we engage in an insidious process of spiritual self-destruction by allowing the well-spring of our apostolic zeal to dry up. As the psalmist tells:

> If the Lord does not build the house,
> in vain do its builders labour;
> if the Lord does not watch over the city,
> in vain does the watchman keep vigil.
>
> Psalm 127

If we set about healing the sick, liberating the oppressed or converting the world without a real knowledge that we are only God's instruments, that our zeal and our talents are his free gift, then we shall soon weary and 'burn out'. If, however, we realize our total dependence on God and are faithful to our communication with him, then we leave him free to use us as he will – to 'give success to the work of our hands' (Psalm 90).

The problems of the person working all day with people are different from those of the person who spends most of the day alone. The difficulty most often encountered by the highly active person is that of 'centring down', of achieving a state of quietness of mind conducive to prayer. Once the cause of this difficulty is recognized it is easier to cope with. We must realize that it is asking a lot of ourselves to rush straight from an engagement to our prayer and not be extremely distracted. This problem may be countered by deliberately leaving our work five minutes earlier so that we have an opportunity to be still. If we arrive five or ten minutes before Mass or whatever service we are attending is due to begin, we are much more likely to be calm and receptive than if we arrive panting a few seconds late. (Having said this I have to admit that I have a perennial tendency to be late, which I still struggle to overcome.) If, despite giving ourselves ample time to be still, we remain distracted by the problems of our work we can only gather them into our prayers and give them to God, asking him to accept us as we are.

The problem of distractions, of course, is not confined to the over-active. Paradoxically, it may be far more difficult to discipline ourselves to pray when we have all day at our disposal than when we are working. Distractions at prayer need only be a problem if we let them be, by which I mean it is not the distractions that are important but our attitude to them. Prayer, as stated so many times, is an act of the will and the value of our prayer depends upon our determination to offer ourselves to God, not upon the whims and fancies of our wayward minds. If we determine to spend a half hour in prayer and do what we can to dispose ourselves to be open to him, then we can be sure that our prayer will ascend like incense in his sight, whatever we may feel. If we find ourselves distracted we should gently return our attention to God, and, if this is just not possible, combat our distractions by making them the subject of our prayer. If a lover's mind is invaded by thoughts of the beloved then let him thank God for the priceless gift of loving and pray that he may be worthy of it. It is the same with worries – if we are unable to leave the problems of our work or home behind us then let us lay them trustingly at the Lord's feet and give him the gift of our restless, aching hearts.

It is not just distractions, of course, that cause problems in prayer. We may find that, however good our dispositions, prayer becomes unutterably boring and difficult to bear. I can remember vividly having literally to hold on to the chair upon which I was sitting to stop myself from walking out of church. When prayer is as difficult as this we may find it helpful to give ourselves a set time – half an hour or less – and promise to remain for that time come what may. If we find ourselves looking at our watches ten or a dozen times in the last five minutes we should not be surprised for time can drag in an unbelievable way. At times of such dryness it may be helpful to read the psalms slowly and meditatively or dwell upon a passage of Scripture, but more often than not we must just give to God all that we have to offer, an agony of boredom. When such dryness besets us it is more important than ever to remember that it is our will and our intention that matters – it is not the boredom of our senses but the fidelity of our hearts that is important.

The question of prayer of petition is one which raises problems for many people, both in whether it is right to ask God for certain things and in how to accept the fact that our requests are frequently not granted. The Scriptures tell us quite clearly that we should ask our Father in Heaven for what we need; the Lord's Prayer is an example of this, as are the familiar words 'ask and you shall receive', 'seek and you shall find', 'knock, and it shall be opened unto you'. As we grow older and more informed in our faith it may be difficult to reconcile the concept of a God who does not interfere in his creation with the prayers of those who ask that the sun should shine on their wedding day or that a loved one dying of cancer should be cured. I have yet to meet a theologian with a real answer to this problem, and suspect that most theologians in moments of crisis call upon God for help as do more simple-minded Christians. I find that my own lack of understanding in this matter does not present a real problem. Although I no longer ask God to alter the weather on my behalf or stay the ravages of disease, I find myself enlisting his help like a foolish child when my car won't start or I have lost something important. The individual's attitude to petitionary prayer will depend much upon his cultural background, his theological understanding and quite simply upon his faith. One aspect of faith is the certainty that God can do anything we ask him – and this I believe; the other side of this belief is the equal certainty that God works for good in all things and therefore asking him for something specific seems unnecessary. My own solution to this problem is simply to 'place' those whom I love at God's feet, certain that he is conscious of my caring, and that he will act for the best in all things.

This attitude has the advantage that it leaves no room for disappointment if God does not grant our desires. If our faith in God is unshakeable we shall be sure that he hears our prayers and that he answers them, though perhaps not in the way we would wish. (Having said this I must admit to the fact that the last time I begged God that my car would start it did!)

A problem which is not uncommon to many people is that of physical weariness during the time of prayer. If our commitments are heavy and we pray early in the morning or late at night we may find ourselves falling asleep as we pray. This weariness need not be a problem and indeed there are times when it can be a help, for there is a certain stilling of the mind in profound physical tiredness that makes it easier to be quiet before God. I have become aware of this recently when, leaving one of my prayer periods until the evening, I have frequently had to fight with the temptation to go to bed because I was so tired. The determination to be faithful on such occasions has many times been rewarded by a greater stillness and peace than I normally achieve. All this is not to say that we should not go to some pains to stay awake during our prayer time. Praying in a stuffy room can be extremely soporific and I personally prefer to be a little cold and remain awake rather than made drowsy by excessive central heating. Position in prayer is of importance in this respect; while it is perfectly possible to pray in bed or sitting in an armchair, if we actually *choose* such cosy sites to wait upon God we are more likely to fall asleep than not, and have only ourselves to blame!

Prayer then, like human dialogue, is an art and it is one which we go on learning all our lives. Not only do we have to learn how to combat the different problems in prayer that arise because of our work or home life, but we have to adapt to the changes that come about in our prayer. At one stage of our lives we may be tongue-tied in God's presence and need a book to help us formulate acts of love and praise; at another we must learn to be quiet and dispense with words and images so that God may deal directly with our souls. While busy and in rude health we may be desperate for time to pray, but when suddenly we find ourselves unemployed or in hospital with nothing to do all day it may be even more difficult to concentrate our minds and wills upon God.

But whatever our problems, be they distractions or the tendency to fall asleep, too many emotions or unbearable boredom, let us cling to the knowledge that it is the will to pray that matters, not what we feel. Last of all, be sure that if you pray for any length of time you *will* have problems but that you are in good company – in the company of saints and sinners of all ages!

CHAPTER XII

The Relationship between Prayer and the Way We Live

Anyone who says 'I love God' and hates his brother, is a liar.

1 John 5 : 19

Jesus tells us in the New Testament that we must worship the Father in Spirit and in Truth and that it is not just those who cry 'Lord, Lord' who will enter the kingdom of heaven but those who do the will of his Father. While it is perfectly true that prayer, our dialogue and personal relationship with God, is the well-spring of all our good works, it is equally true that if our prayer does not lead us to a deepening love of man and a conversion of life then something is seriously wrong. The prophet Isaiah has some powerful words to say on the subject. In chapter I the word of the Lord is addressed to the people of Sodom and Gomorrah:

> What are your endless sacrifices to me?
>   says Yahweh.
> I am sick of holocausts of rams
>   and the fat of calves.
> The blood of bulls and goats revolts me.
> When you come to present yourself before me,

who asked you to trample over my courts?
Bring me your worthless offerings no more,
the smoke of them fills me with disgust.
New Moons, sabbaths, assemblies –
I cannot endure festival and solemnity.
Your New Moons and your pilgrimages
I hate with all my soul.
They lie heavy on me,
I am tired of bearing them.
When you stretch out your hands
I turned my eyes away.
You may multiply your prayers,
I shall not listen.
Your hands are covered with blood,
wash, make yourselves clean.
Take your wrong-doing out of my sight.
Cease to do evil.
Learn to do good,
search for justice,
help the oppressed,
be just to the orphan,
plead for the widow.

Isaiah 1: 11–17

The sentiments expressed in this passage are repeated many times throughout both Old and New Testaments but especially in the writings of the prophets and the letters of the apostles John and James. The prophet Micah captures the essence of these teachings in this passage:

This is what Yahweh asks of you:
only this, to act justly,

to love tenderly
and to walk humbly with your God.

Micah 6:8

But what, we may ask, do these words, written over two thousand years ago, have to do with us, people of a different race, civilization and culture? Perhaps the following 'modern' version of the passage from Isaiah will make the answer clearer:

What are your endless religious services to me?
says the Lord.
I am sick of your plain chant and your folk
    hymns.
The smell of votive candles revolts me.
When you come to worship on Sunday,
Who asked you to come into my house?
Stop burning incense to me at High Mass
and Benediction,
its smoke fills me with disgust.
I cannot endure
your Holy Days of Obligation, your Days of
    Recollection and your Pilgrimages
I hate with all my soul.
They lie heavy on me,
I am tired of bearing them.
When you stretch out your hands
I turn my eyes away.
You may make Novenas and say Rosaries but
    I shall not listen.
You are guilty of the death of my people,
so wash, make yourself clean.
Take your wrongdoing out of my sight.

Cease to do evil.
Learn to do good,
Search for justice,
help the oppressed, the poor, the starving, the
    elderly, the lonely, the imprisoned,
be just to the orphan, the unmarried mother, the
    mentally and physically disabled,
plead for the widow, the refugee and the
    immigrant.

If this interpretation of Scripture seems blasphe-
mous it is not intended to be so; if it is thought-
provoking then it has achieved its purpose. The
prophet, of course, is not condemning worship and
liturgy *per se* but its performance by those who
commit grave injustice in their everyday life and
then come shamelessly to offer sacrifice. If Isaiah
were with us today he would not condemn our
worship but he would surely challenge those who
from Monday to Friday run unjust businesses,
extort excessive rents or abuse the innocent, and
then come piously to church in their Sunday best
to take their place in the front pew.

Seen in this light, what I say should seen reason-
able. These harsh words obviously refer to dictators
and murderers, criminals and frauds; they do not
concern 'us'. Or do they? This is where the crunch
comes, for most Christians are convinced that they
are doing their humble best to serve God and man.
If they were *not* thus convinced they would either
do more or cease to go to church altogether.

In the long run, of course, God will be our judge

as to whether we have acted justly and loved tenderly, and we have no right to judge one another lest we ourselves be judged. What seems, however, to be perfectly fair is to voice aloud the very uncomfortable questions that disturb my own peace of soul. I do not know the answers to many of the questions, but I have a growing conviction that far too many of us are living a tepid watered-down Christianity which bears only a faint resemblance to the hard message preached by Christ. When we really examine the implications of the Christian message it comes as no surprise that Christ was arrested as a disturber of the peace and that they crucified him to silence him. Of course the incredible thing about Christianity is that the mere killing of the man Jesus didn't silence him at all, for his message has lived on for two thousand years, and countless thousands have died because they proclaimed it. Nor has the martyrdom of Christ's followers stopped, for their blood flows daily in oppressive regimes the world over. In the words of T. S. Eliot:

And the Son of Man was not crucified once for
    all,
The blood of martyrs not shed once for all,
The lives of the Saints not given once for all:
But the Son of Man is crucified always
And these shall be Martyrs and Saints.
        T. S. Eliot, *Choruses from The Rock*, VI

In his farewell discourse at the Last Supper Christ tells his disciples:

I give you a new commandment:
love one another;
just as I have loved you,
you also must love one another.
By this love you have for one another,
everyone will know you are my disciples.

John 13 : 34f.

If this was the central theme of Jesus' message, that
we should love one another, how is it that it led
to his crucifixion? To understand why they killed
him we must analyse two things: what did Jesus
mean by love and whom did he mean us to love?
If we are to understand what Jesus meant by love
we must study not only his words but his example,
and we must examine the teaching of those who
knew him personally or followed close after him.
In St John's Gospel we have Jesus' teaching on love
contained in his discourse on the vine and its
branches. He tells the disciples:

As the Father has loved me,
so I have loved you.
Remain in my love.
If you keep my commandments
you will remain in my love,
just as I have kept my Father's commandments
and remain in his love.
I have told you this
so that my own joy may be in you
and your joy be complete.
This is my commandment:

love one another
as I have loved you.
A man can have no greater love
than to lay down his life for his friends.

John 15: 9–13

From this we learn three main truths: that Jesus
has loved us just as God loves him; that if we are
to remain in this love then we must keep his
commandments just as he has kept his father's
commandments; and that the greatest demand of
love is that a man lay down his life for his friends.
If we are to understand the way in which Jesus
fulfilled his Father's commandments we must look
at the pattern of his life, a life lived in poverty, in
obscurity, in the service of others. Throughout his
ministry Jesus was at pains to teach his disciples
that their lives were to be ones of service to the
needy. Not only did he spend all his own active
life in preaching and healing, but he who was their
master washed their feet so as to drive home for
ever the message that love means service of others.

This much of Jesus' teaching is not hard to grasp,
even if it is not easy to put into practice. Service
and care of those whom we humanly love is to some
extent built into our make-up – the care of a mother
for her child, of a lover for his beloved. The difficulty comes when we examine *who* it is that Jesus
tells us to love.

Here we must turn to the familiar story of the
good Samaritan, the parable which Jesus told in
response to the question: 'And who is my neigh-

bour?' We do well to remember the setting of this story, told in Luke's Gospel:

There was a lawyer who, to disconcert him, stood up and said to him, 'Master, what must I do to inherit eternal life?' He said to him, 'What is written in the Law? What do you read there?' He replied 'You must love the Lord your God with all your heart, with all your soul, with all your strength, and with all your mind, and your neighbour as yourself.' 'You have answered right,' said Jesus. 'Do this and life is yours.'

But the man was anxious to justify himself and said to Jesus, 'And who is my neighbour?'

Luke 10: 25–29

There follows the well-known story of the man who fell among thieves who beat him up, stole his money and left him to die by the roadside.

This man is a symbol of every man, woman and child in need; he represents the sick, the imprisoned, the lonely, the oppressed, the hungry. As the man lay bleeding in the ditch two men of the church went by, men who by their very calling should have ministered to those in need, but we are told that they passed by on the other side of the road. But then there came a stranger to the district, and it was he who was 'moved with compassion', dressed the man's wounds, carried him to an inn and paid for his care. The Samaritan is specially chosen as someone who had no blood relationship with the injured man, no shared nationality and no professional or religious obligation to the needy. His act was not the instinctive love a mother has for her child, nor yet the love of a man for someone of his own social class, colour or race. Still less was it the love of someone dedicated to the service of others – the doctor, the nurse or the social worker. No, he was a foreign traveller, a man without obligation to stop and even less to give his time, labour and money to a man he did not know. This is the man whom Christ portrays as he who is neighbour to another.

What, then, are we to learn from this story, from the message to the pharisee to 'Go and do likewise'? It is the principle of gratuitous love for all men, love that knows no barriers, that is not limited to friends and family, fellow countrymen or those with whom we feel a common bond. It is the command to love everyone but especially those who most need our love: the poor, the sick, the old and the rejected.

This parable is so familiar to us that we have ceased to be upset by it; but the demands it makes upon us are terrifying. It is a demand to open our hearts to a global caring, to break down the barriers which limit our love to those in our family or whom we find it easy to love. It is a demand that is pure dynamite to our way of life as civilized people of the Western world, for it is not possible to consider the starving of Biafra, the dispossessed of Cambodia or the tortured of Latin America as brother and continue in the same way as our forefathers. Such demands turn our value system and

P.F.P.—F

accepted norms of behaviour completely upside down.

I learned today that there are two types of slipped disc; one is known as a hard lesion because it comes on quite suddenly, the other as a soft lesion because it comes on gradually, first as a mild discomfort, then as a persistent ache and finally as a violent pain which immobilizes the sufferer. The long-term results are the same: chronic pain which leads to an alteration in the way of life of the sufferer. After a while he learns to live with the pain, but life is never quite the same again and he is always liable to suffer an acute attack. It seems to me that the recognition of our brotherhood with the oppressed is not unlike the onset of a slipped disc. The onset may be sudden or gradual, but once it has happened there is no going back and life is never as comfortable as it was before.

The implications of the concept of universal brotherhood are so wide and so devastating that most people are unable to assimilate them at once. Those who do assimilate them behave like St Francis of Assisi and, stripping themselves of their possessions in one dramatic gesture, go off to live with the poor. For those of us who do not have the simplicity and clarity of vision of St Francis the process is slower, more complex and infinitely less radical.

Since we know that all things are a gift, then we must acknowledge that this recognition of our brotherhood with the poor is God's gift and, like the gift of faith, it is one that we cannot communicate to others unless they are open to receive it. All we can do (and it is much) is examine our own life style in the light of this new understanding and act in accordance with the degree of *metanoia* or change of heart that we have been granted.

The problems involved in this process are many and involve consideration not only of our own needs and way of life but of the whole structure of the society in which we live. This consideration, if we are open to it, can lead to gradual deepening in understanding of the way in which we are conditioned by our upbringing, our education, friends and milieu, and such an understanding should lead to a realization of two factors. The first is that we are in a very real sense prisoners of our society, and the second is that it is within our power to break free from this servitude. That such a process of liberation is easy or painless I do not for one moment pretend. It is both difficult and painful, but the liberation of spirit that results from this breaking away is more than reward for the pain involved.

Let us consider first the intellectual process involved and then the practical consequences of any conclusions reached thereby. The first premise to consider is that all people are equally sons of God, and that they all have the right to the basic necessities of life. Now if the reader does *not* accept this premise, which is written into the United Nations Declaration on Human Rights and is squarely based on Christ's teaching 'You shall love your neighbour as yourself', then it is not worth reading further. If, however, this premise is accepted then certain things are consequent upon it. There follows the question: 'Do all men receive their basic human rights?' The answer to this is patently 'No'. In this curious age in which we live there is scarcely a corner of the globe that is not exposed to us in the comfort of our own homes. We may, if we wish, see films of children who are dying of starvation, of men and women fleeing from gunfire, and we may listen to first-hand accounts of torture and unjust imprisonment. The evidence of the hunger, illiteracy, inadequate health care and oppression of millions of people in our world is so great that if we are not aware of it we are either consciously or unconsciously shutting our eyes and ears to the evidence that surrounds us.

Awareness of the suffering of others, of course, is one thing. The realization that we have a possibility, even a duty, to alleviate that suffering is quite another. Yet a further step in deepening our relationship with others is to understand the degree to which we as individuals and members of a community bear responsibility for their sufferings. It would seem that for most people this development of understanding occurs in a step-wise progression. It begins with an awareness of the existence of suffering, moves on to a desire to help the sufferer and continues with an act of charity, perhaps a small donation in response to a radio appeal or to a moving sermon from a visiting missionary. There are many people who never go beyond this stage, and it would be presumptuous to judge them.

Donations to charity, small and large, alleviate the sufferings of many thousands of people, and the Christian tradition of alms-giving is a long one. Charity is good, but there is a further stage of commitment. Most of us who give to the needy give out of the surplus of our wealth but not to the extent that we change our standard of living in any significant way.

The second stage of commitment to the needy is the giving of time. This is a much deeper degree of involvement, not only because most people are extremely busy with their work, their family or both, but because with this spending of time there is an inevitable degree of emotional involvement. It is far easier to send a cheque for five pounds to the Society for the Blind than it is to go once a week to read to a blind neighbour. In a different area, there is a great difference in terms of commitment in buying Christmas cards from Amnesty International and in joining together with neighbours to form a group which writes letters to prisoners of conscience and those who maltreat them. However, once we take the step of personal involvement as opposed to alms-giving we are embarking upon the road which leads to loving neighbour as self. This is a road which is hard and very long, and we must learn to be gentle as well as honest with ourselves and others in the question of how far we personally are called to travel down this road at any stage of our lives. God does not ask us to neglect our work or our families in order to serve others; at least he does not call many people in this way. That he calls some to abandon home, father, mother and career to follow in his footsteps is abundantly clear in the gospels. What we have to examine, however, is the conviction that we have no time at all to spare for the needy and no money in excess of our needs.

It is at this stage that we have to re-examine our ideas of what is essential to our wellbeing, and it is here that things start to become uncomfortable. Looking back over the past twenty years of my own life I can see the gradual progression from my life as an undergraduate when I lived happily in one room with a gas ring, an inexpensive gramophone and a bicycle, to the years after qualifying as a doctor when I lived in the large house that went with my job, owned a stereophonic record-player, a tape-recorder, a typewriter, a pedigree dog, a Triumph motorcar and a cottage by the sea. At this particular stage in my life I not only considered all these possessions essential to my survival as a hard-worked doctor, but I emigrated in search of shorter hours, domestic help and a house with a swimming pool! It has taken me many years to learn that I was much happier in the earlier days. It is, of course, the old story: money does not bring happiness.

The point I am endeavouring to make, however, is the slightly more subtle one that, with all the good will in the world, we deceive ourselves into believing that the luxuries which are now common-place in our society are in fact necessities. We become conditioned, quite unawares, to believe that a good quality record-player, a colour television, a pre-dinner drink and a holiday abroad are essential to our life as civilized Westerners. Now I am not for one moment saying that any of these things is intrinsically evil, nor that I myself do not enjoy each item I have mentioned. The question I am asking, of myself as much as anyone else, is by what right I enjoy these luxuries while my neighbour goes hungry, cold or without medical care?

Here we come right back to the question 'who is my neighbour?' It is here that we must face a very difficult and disturbing truth. If we have any right to call ourselves Christians we must include in our definition of neighbour not only the lady next door and the under-privileged of our immediate neighbourhood, but also the hungry, the sick and the oppressed in other lands. The horrid truth is that the starving children of Biafra and the tortured prisoners of Latin America are as far away from us as our cheque book and our telephone. This country is full of organizations which ask for a share in our wealth to send to the hungry and alleviate the distress of the lonely, disabled and imprisoned.

A quite different concept from that of sharing with the needy our wealth of time, talent and money is that of our corporate and individual responsibility for the misfortunes of others. Let us take a very simple example which illustrates the way in which the economy of the wealthier nations is inextricably linked with that of the poorer ones. The majority of people in this country drink coffee at least once a day. Many people (including myself) prefer it to tea and certainly to water, and it is indeed a most comforting and stimulating beverage. The coffee we drink is grown mainly in Latin America, particularly in Brazil and Colombia. It comes to us more often than not in convenient tin canisters which are light, easy to open and keep the product fresh and palatable. The tin for these containers is also a product of the so-called 'third world', being mined in the South American country of Bolivia. Now let us for a moment look beyond the shelves of the supermarket where we buy our coffee and think of the people involved in the growing of the coffee and the mining of the tin. Let us think of them not as nameless, faceless men in a continent twelve thousand miles away but as 'neighbours', in the same way that the farmer's wife from whom we might buy our eggs is a neighbour.

The life style of these 'neighbours', however, is very different from that of our British ones. They live in houses that have no light and no proper sanitation, and their children, barefoot and pot-bellied from malnutrition, are lucky if they go to school. The following is an extract from a book which describes the conditions of life of a Brazilian slum-dweller:

It seems that the slaughterhouse threw kerosene on their garbage dump so that the *favelado* (slum-dweller) would not look for meat to eat. I didn't have any breakfast and walked around half dizzy. The state of hunger is worse than that of alcohol. The daze of alcohol makes us sing, but the one of hunger makes us shake. I know how horrible it is to have only air in the stomach.

From *Beyond All Pity*, by
Carolina Maria de Jesus;
quoted in *The Radical Bible*

Our other 'neighbour' involved in the coffee we drink is the Bolivian tin-miner. A recent survey has shown that it is rare for these miners to live beyond the age of forty because they die from silicosis since conditions of work are such that they inhale a dangerous quantity of dust. A Colombian bishop writes:

When we look at our Bolivian reality with the eyes of the Gospel, we find ourselves confronted with the spectacle of a chronic and heart-rending dehumanization: a country of immense resources sunk in backwardness and under-development; a country living in under-consumption with the lowest per capita income of all Latin America, 'the cemeteries of the miners', macabre witnesses of generations sacrificed in the prime of life, leaving, after eight or ten years of production, their skeletons and families of orphans and widows abandoned to the most abject helplessness, while the minerals extracted with the sacrifice of their lives enrich a certain few and strengthen the industry and finances of the rich nations of the earth; three million peasants, the basic population of the nation, still set apart by illiteracy and poverty and treated as mere disposable objects by political bossism and by the insensitive bureaucracy.

Bishop Mortimer Arias,
quoted in The Radical Bible

Our first reaction to this picture of our 'neighbours' is surely one of horror and leads us to ask why these men are not paid a living wage and why their conditions of work are not better. The answer is simple enough. Money. If the coffee workers were paid more and the tin-miners protected from the silicosis which kills them, the costs of production of a tin of coffee would go up. These increased production costs would mean a lower margin of profit for the companies that buy raw coffee and market the finished product, unless they passed the increased costs on to the consumer, thereby raising the price of coffee. Perhaps the price would rise so high that many people would no longer be able to drink it every day and the whole pattern of their lives would be altered. This is indeed a daunting prospect, yet we must ask ourselves what right we have to use a product that is within our reach, in large part, because those who produce it are not paid a living wage. We may have to accept that something that we have long regarded as a basic commodity is, in fact, a luxury which we have only enjoyed at relatively low prices because of the exploitation of those who produce it.

The other question raised is, of course, the profit

margin of those concerned in the marketing of the product. This brings us to consider the ethics of what are known as the Multi-National Corporations. These are immense industrial enterprises which own the raw materials in many developing countries, control the wage paid to those who work to produce them and the price at which they are marketed. A detailed study of this matter is outside my competence, but it would reveal the basic truth that it is not only the poor nations who need the rich nations to help them 'develop' their resources but the rich nations who need the poor ones in order to maintain the high standard of living to which they have become assustomed. One must ask, too, who in the poor nations gains from their 'development'. It is rarely the poor.

There are many other examples of the way in which the lives of ordinary people in both the 'developed' and the 'developing' nations are manipulated by big business. The arms trade is a classic example; the sale of arms is a highly profitable business and it is an appalling truth that many men and women in Europe and the USA live in great luxury on the profits they make from selling arms to smaller nations which are fighting over the redistribution of wealth among their citizens. Certainly the armies involved 'need' the arms that are sold to them, but it is equally true to say that those in the armaments business 'need' these wars to maintain their standard of living.

If we accept the truth of these statements, that the present *status quo* of unfair distribution of the world's goods is not merely tolerated but deliberately maintained by certain elements in our society, what should be our response as Christians? This is again a question that I do not feel competent to answer, for we must each act according to our conscience. It is, I think, fair to say that we have a duty to 'inform' our conscience as far as we are able and to act accordingly. If we do this we shall initiate, however slowly, a process of change. Some will be moved to pray in greater earnest, others to give alms, others to work in some way for the deprived. Still others will feel called to speak out against injustice and to challenge the existing order of society and the injustice they see within it.

We are not asked to act beyond our physical, intellectual or emotional capabilities, nor against our consciences; but we are called by the very fact of our baptism to arise from our lethargy and attempt to love our neighbour as God loves him.

Do not model yourselves on the behaviour of the world around you, but let your behaviour change, modelled by your new mind. This is the only way to discover the will of God and know what is good, what it is that God wants, what is the perfect thing to do.

Romans 12:2

Wake up from your sleep,
rise from the dead,
and Christ will shine on you.

Ephesians 5:14

CHAPTER XIII

The Effects of Prayer

I live now not with my own life but with the
life of Christ who lives in me.

Galatians 2:20

People who devote time to the practice of prayer
will sooner or later be asked the question: 'What
does prayer do for you?' This is in no way easy to
answer, and yet it is an honest question and as such
deserves an honest answer. In replying we can only
say what we believe prayer does for us personally
and what, in theory, should happen to any person
who takes prayer seriously.

If prayer is communication with God, then the
first and most important thing that it does is to
open us to the grace of God, to his power to transform us into his likeness. The manner in which this
occurs is impossible to define clearly, for we are
dealing not with a scientific process but with the
mysterious workings of the Spirit. As happens so
frequently when we speak of man's relationship
with God, we must turn to poetry, to imagery and
metaphor, because these are the tools of language
most suited to convey the mystery of spiritual experience. It is perhaps not surprising that a fav-

ourite scriptural image for the portrayal of God's relationship with man is that of the potter and the clay vessels he makes. If we have never done so it is worth going to watch a potter at work on his wheel, for it is only then that we can fully appreciate how a vessel of one shape can be totally transformed into another simply by the skilled moulding of a craftsman's hands.

The prophet Jeremiah speaks of how God told him to do just this:

> The word that was addressed to Jeremiah by Yahweh, 'Get up and make your way down to the potter's house; there I shall let you hear what I have to say.' So I went down to the potter's house; and there he was, working at the wheel. And whenever the vessel he was making came out wrong, as happens with the clay handled by potters, he would start afresh and work it into another vessel, as potters do. Then this word of Yahweh was addressed to me, 'House of Israel, can not I do to you what this potter does? – it is Yahweh who speaks. Yes, as the clay is in the potter's hand, so you are in mine, House of Israel.'
>
> Jeremiah 18: 1–6

This refashioning by God of those who are prepared to yield to his touch is one of the most fascinating features of Christian history and of the lives of the saints. The dramatic Damascus road encounter of Saul, the persecutor of the Christians, and his transformation into the apostle Paul, witnesses to the power of the Spirit of God which 'blows where it will' and can change a sinner into a great saint. Mary Magdalene, Augustine of Hippo, the English Benedictine martyr Alban Roe, all sinners turned saint, speak to us of the power of God to change the hearts of men.

These saints are outstanding in the history of the Church, but if we enquire into the lives of many apparently ordinary people of our time we shall see that God's transforming power is ever at work. This power to effect radical change in the lives of those who co-operate with his grace should be to us a constant source of wonder and encouragement, so that we never lose heart because of our frailty and sin.

Prayer leads not only to a deepening knowledge of God and his ways but to an increase in self-understanding. The recognition of our particular weaknesses of character is basic to growth in the spiritual life, for self-awareness and the realization of how far we fall short of the Christian ideal leads us to acknowledge our nothingness before God, and that without him we can do nothing. With this increase of self-awareness there must also come the power to accept and love ourselves in spite of our faults. If we cannot accept our weakness we shall never learn to be patient and compassionate with others, and the man who is unable to love himself will not be capable of loving another. This concept of loving ourselves may seem strange, but it is another way of saying that we must appreciate the fact that God loves us and that our duty to love ourselves stems from this fact. We find the image of the potter and his vessel also in the prophet Isaiah:

> Can it argue with the man who fashioned it,
> one vessel among earthen vessels?
> Does the clay say to its fashioner, 'What are
> you making?',
> does the thing he shaped say, 'You have no
> skill'?
> Woe to him who says to a father, 'What have
> you begotten?'
> or to a woman, 'To what have you given birth?'
>   Isaiah 45: 9–10

We shall find it necessary all our lives to work to achieve a balance between accepting those imperfections in ourselves which we cannot change, whilst at the same time striving to co-operate with God's grace to overcome them. The writings of St Paul reveal especially clearly his appreciation of the change that can be brought about in all men by the grace of God, for Paul not only speaks frequently of his own conversion but reminds his disciples of the dissipation of their lives before they received the grace of conversion. Particularly comforting is Paul's understanding of how God works through human frailty:

> ... to stop me from getting too proud I was given a thorn in the flesh, an angel of Satan to beat

me and stop me from getting too proud. About
this thing, I have pleaded with the Lord three
times for it to leave me, but he has said, 'My
grace is enough for you: my power is at its best
in weakness'.

2 Corinthians 12: 7–9

The way in which God chooses the weak and the
sinful to be his instruments may at first sight seem
strange, but this is a pattern which runs throughout both Old and New Testament. We find that
God chooses the frail not by chance but precisely
so that his power may be the more clearly manifest
in them. A study of the calling of the prophets of
the Old Testament is especially revealing in this
respect. When God called Moses to lead the Israel-
ites out of their slavery in Egypt Moses protested
that he was unsuitable – as indeed he was, for he
had just killed an Egyptian and was on the run
from the authorities. Moses says to God, 'Who am
I to go to Pharaoh and bring the sons of Israel out
of Egypt?' God answers with the promise that he
gives to all those who step out into the unknown
in answer to his call:

I shall be with you.

Exodus 3: 12

The call of the prophet Isaiah reveals a similar
sense of unworthiness. Isaiah sees a vision in which
the Lord appears in all his glory, surrounded by
angels:

The foundations of the threshold shook with the voice of the one who cried out, and the temple was filled with smoke. I said:
'What a wretched state I am in! I am lost, for I am a man of unclean lips and I live among a people of unclean lips, and my eyes have looked at the King, Yahweh Sabaoth.'

It is not Isaiah who makes himself worthy to be God's messenger but the power of the Lord which cleanses him:

Then one of the seraphs flew to me, holding in his hand a live coal which he had taken from the altar with a pair of tongs. With this he touched my mouth and said:
'See now, this has touched your lips, your sin is taken away, your iniquity is purged.'

It is only then that, cleansed of his sin, Isaiah feels able to answer God's call:

Then I heard the voice of the Lord saying:
'Whom shall I send? Who will be our messenger?'
I answered, 'Here I am, send me.'

Isaiah 6: 4–9

God, then, calls those whom he chooses, and if they accept his invitation and co-operate with his grace by prayer and conformity to his will he can do great things in them. But man is ever free and his 'fiat', his 'yes', must be a continuing response, a process of constant consent to what God is asking. An attitude of listening to God, which is the essence of prayer, is essential to the knowledge of what is the will of God for us. Although we can guess, perhaps with a high degree of accuracy, what the future pattern of our lives may be we can never know it for certain, so if we wish to be available to the Spirit of God we must remain ever open to the possibility that he is going to ask something quite unexpected of us.

This attitude of being prepared for the unexpected is not unlike that cultivated by the mothers of small children and by doctors in emergency hospitals. The mother knows that if she turns her back for one moment she risks finding her child with his fingers in an electrical socket or reaching for a saucepan of boiling water. Similarly for the doctor: hour after hour of routine work in a casualty department is suddenly interrupted by the arrival of a seriously injured motorcyclist, a child who has taken poison, a woman with haemorrhage, and so on. Quite literally the doctor knows not the day nor the hour when his immediate response will be necessary to save a life.

And so it is with our openness to God. We must be ever alert to the people we meet and situations which occur, for the requests he makes often come in a totally unexpected form. This openness can only be achieved by listening to God in regular prayer, by 'pondering' on his word in the Scriptures and by reflecting upon the way he has revealed his purpose to us in the past. Much of our understanding of God's action in our lives is achieved in hindsight. When a particular crisis or event in our life has passed we cry out in astonishment like Jacob, 'The Lord is in this place and I never knew it' (Genesis 28: 16). Like the wise virgins we must await the bridegroom's coming with our lamps trimmed, certain of his coming but acknowledging our ignorance of when that moment will be (cf., Matthew 25).

This attitude of expectancy towards the demands of God will be reflected in our lives in two main ways: in availability to our neighbour and in the knowledge of the ephemeral nature of human life – that we are ever pilgrims on this earth. The essence of Christian living is not that we must pray to God and be good to our neighbour but that *from* our prayer there will arise the awareness of our neighbour's needs, the recognition of our brotherhood with him, the desire to be of service and the strength to give from our own material and spiritual fullness to the less fortunate. Herein lies the mystery of grace and human freedom. Grace is God's gift to men, giving them the possibility of sharing in the Divine Life. This gift is freely given; it may be accepted or rejected. Acceptance requires that we lay ourselves open to his transforming power, to be refashioned as clay in the hand of the potter, to be tried in the furnace 'as silver is tried' (Psalm 65). Rejection is the beginning of the process which culminates in what is described in the Old Testament as 'hardness of heart', and it renders a man progressively less open to love, less malleable in the hands of God, less available to his neighbour.

The message that love of God must find its expression in the service of neighbour is found frequently in the pages of the Scriptures and is expressed in a forthright manner in the Epistle of St John:

> Anyone who says, 'I love God', and hates his brother, is a liar, since a man who does not love the brother that he can see cannot love God, whom he has never seen.
>
> 1 John 4:20

It is precisely because we cannot see God that we can only know that our prayer is valid by the effect it has upon our lives, by the way we treat our neighbour. This is not a conversion of the worship of God into a philosophy of the service of man, for it is an essential tenet of Christianity that the two are inseparable. In his discourse on the final judgement Christ tells his disciples that those who will be saved are those who ministered to him when he entered their lives in the guise of the hungry, the thirsty, the sick and the imprisoned. Those who fail to heed the cries of the needy will on the last day hear the words:

> 'I tell you solemnly, in so far as you neglected to do this to one of the least of these, you neglected to do it to me.'
> And they will go away to eternal punishment, and the virtuous to eternal life.
>
> Matthew 25:45f.

This concept of Christ present in all men is basic to our understanding of the presence of the Risen Christ in our world. This is the Good News of Christianity, that God became man, and taking on our frail human nature lived a life of service which culminated in the laying down of his life for others; but because he was the Son of God death had no dominion over him and he lives for ever in our midst. Ours must not be a religion of the worship of idols but of the Father God, whom no man has ever seen nor will see in this life, and of his Son who lives among us, incarnate in us and in our brothers by the indwelling of the Holy Spirit whose breath gives life to our souls.

An attitude of openness to the demands of God expressed in the needs of our neighbour leads naturally to an awareness of the ultimate demand that may be made upon us, that of our life. While the knowledge of the inevitability of death is a common human experience, the ability to accept and welcome the fact that it may happen at any time comes with spiritual maturity. It has, however, become somehow unfashionable, even ill-mannered, to speak of the inevitability of death and of our total ignorance of when we, or those we love, will die. This is, not unnaturally, especially true of young people who take it for granted that they have many years of life ahead of them. Lucky indeed are those who are startled out of this complacency by the death of a friend or a near-fatal illness of their own.

Awareness of the possibility that we may die at

any moment is in no way the same as a morbid fear of death. The man or woman who prays constantly and lives ever attuned to the voice of God has no fear of death. When all we desire is what God wills for us then good health and long life are no longer essential to peace and happiness. Such a person genuinely does not care whether he lives for another forty years or dies tomorrow. If that is what God wants, then it is what his disciple wants. This attitude of mind accounts for the deep serenity of men and women of prayer. Theirs is a joy which no one can take from them, for it derives not from the things of this world but of the next.

It must be understood in this context that such acceptance of the designs of God is an act of the will and does not necessarily render the believer exempt from fear of pain and death. Deep faith in God should be, and usually is, a great help in facing the prospect of death, either one's own or that of a loved one. Nevertheless, however great a person's faith it will always be difficult to accept the fact of a fatal illness, and belief in the value of suffering provides no relief for pain and incapacity. The inevitability of fear and distress notwithstanding, men and women of prayer usually have the faith required to face pain and death with a greater degree of serenity than does the unbeliever.

With the understanding that on earth we have no lasting city comes a degree of detachment from things material. As our faith deepens so does our trust in God. While we may not be graced with the courage to travel without spare shoes or tunic, our faith should free us from the emotional and physical insecurity of those who feel obliged to provide for every possible contingency in their lives. So much of the spiritual sickness of our society is based upon insecurity. When a strike is threatened we fill our store cupboards with provisions because we are afraid of running short, but we fail to see that our panic hoarding infects our neighbour and so helps to create the very scarcity of which we are afraid. Faith in the loving providence of God, which can only be generated by knowledge of him in prayer, allows us to relax into his hands, secure in the certainty that he who guides the sun and the stars can guide the faltering steps of our leaders and fellow countrymen. Herein lies not a foolish refusal to join in the fight for the survival of the fittest but the Christian virtue of hope.

Hope, like all the theological virtues, is a gift of God and is an 'effect' of prayer. Unlike *expectation*, with which it is often confused and which is based upon what we can see as a possible outcome of any situation, hope is based upon the unshakeable belief that God can and will bring about the unlikely, the humanly impossible, however black the future looks. It is hope that gives prisoners of conscience the courage to withstand torture, to sing in solitary confinement and to tolerate a life spent year after year in concentration camps from which there is no apparent possibility of release. Hope is the virtue which enables the relatives of the incurably ill to face the future, the oppressed to believe in the possibility of liberation, the Christian to be opti-

mistic in the face of rising inflation and unemploy-
ment. It is not a childish refusal to face facts, but a
child-like trust that the Father's love will not fail
and that he has the power to bring good out of
evil, new life out of death. In the words of Charles
de Foucauld, *Jésu est le maître de l'impossible* –
Jesus is the master of the impossible!

The ultimate expression of hope is our belief in
life after death, and it is this conviction that gives
deep meaning to the lives of all Christians. This is
a belief based entirely upon faith and hope, and it
is the cornerstone of our whole way of life. If there
were no life after death there would be no hope
for those whose life is, humanly speaking, a failure
– the insane, the brain-damaged and so on. It is,
however, the glory of our faith that this life is but
a preparation for a life of union with God and that
we have nothing to fear from those who have power
to kill our bodies:

> But the souls of the virtuous are in the hands
>   of God,
> no torment shall ever touch them.
> In the eyes of the unwise, they did appear to
>   die,
> their going looked like a disaster,
> their leaving us, like annihilation;
> but they are in peace.
>
> Wisdom 3 : 1–3

The Christian belief in an after-life is the basis for
the doctrine of the Mystical Body and the Com-

munion of Saints. This doctrine is explained at length by St Paul:

> Just as a human body, though it is made up of many parts, is a single unit because all these parts, though many, make one body, so it is with Christ. In the one Spirit we were all baptized, Jews as well as Greeks, slaves as well as citizens, and one Spirit was given to us all to drink.
> Nor is the body to be identified with any one of its many parts. If the foot were to say, 'I am not a hand and so I do not belong to the body', would that mean that it stopped being part of the body? If the ear were to say, 'I am not an eye, and so I do not belong to the body', would that mean that it was not a part of the body? If your whole body was just one eye, how would you hear anything? If it was just one ear, how would you smell anything? ...
> Now you together are Christ's body; but each of you is a different part of it.
>
> 1 Corinthians 12: 12ff.

Paul's concept of the Mystical Body of Christ includes not only all the living who are in communion (whether consciously or not) with Christ but also those members who have died. This is a belief which adds a whole new dimension of comfort and strength to those who accept it. Not only does it bring home to us the truth that separation from our dead loved ones is but a temporary affair, but it gives us a sense of family that extends horizontally across the world and vertically through time. Caryll Houselander, a British laywoman and writer who died in 1954, writes of a vision she once had in the Underground.

I was in an underground train, a crowded train in which all sorts of people jostled together, sitting and strap-hanging – workers of every description going home at the end of the day. Quite suddenly I saw with my mind, but as vividly as a wonderful picture, Christ in them all. But I saw more than that; not only was Christ in every one of them, living in them, dying in them, rejoicing in them, sorrowing in them – but because he was in them, and because they were here, the whole world was here too, here in this underground train; not only the world as it was at that moment, not only all the people in all the countries of the world, but all those people who had lived in the past, and all those yet to come.

I came out into the street and walked for a long time in the crowds. It was the same here, on every side, in every passer-by, everywhere – Christ ...

I saw too the reverence that everyone must have for a sinner; instead of condoning his sin, which is in reality his utmost sorrow, one must comfort Christ who is suffering in him. And this reverence must be paid even to those sinners whose souls seem to be dead, because it is Christ, who is the life of the soul, who is dead in them: they are his tombs, and Christ in the tomb is potentially the risen Christ. For the same reason, no one of us who has fallen into mortal sin himself must ever lose hope …

After a few days the 'vision' faded. People looked the same again, there was no longer the same shock of insight for me each time I was face to face with another human being. Christ was hidden again; indeed, through the years to come I would have to seek for him, and usually I would find him in others – and still more in myself – only through a deliberate and blind act of faith. But if the 'vision' had faded, the knowledge had not; on the contrary, that knowledge, touched by a ray of the Holy Spirit, is like a tree touched by the sun – it puts out leaf and flowers, bearing fruit and blossom from splendour to splendour.

Caryll Houselander,
A Rocking Horse Catholic

I have always found this passage intensely moving, and my own sense of communion with the 'saints' has been greatly strengthened by the experience of attending the Divine Office. In the monastery where I joined in the monk's worship for nearly two years, it was the custom to commemorate each day not only the saint whose 'feast' it was but the less famous saints who had died on the same day and also the deceased members of the community. Each morning I 'made the acquaintance' of holy men and women, martyrs and virgins from early post-Christian times to our own. It was particularly moving to hear daily the names of English priests and laymen hanged, beheaded or starved to death during the sixteenth and seventeeth centuries. The realization that many had died for the faith in York, only a few miles from where I lived, gave me a great sense of union with them, and people like St Alban Roe, who was a monk of Dieulouard, the original foundation of Ampleforth Abbey, and St Margaret Clitheroe, the butcher's wife martyred in York, have become in a very real sense my friends.

As our appreciation of the transcendent deepens, the divisions between the spiritual and the temporal world become less clearly demarcated, and as I 'met' Bernard of Clairvaux, Anselm of Bec, Teresa of Avila, Alban Roe or Margaret Clitheroe I came to know them as real people who had loved and laughed, wept and suffered just as I do. Because of our shared human experience and life of grace we are united by a bond which death cannot sever. Rupert Brooke, poet and soldier who was killed in the First World War, has captured this sense of our unbroken link with the dead in a poem:

> These hearts were woven of human joys and
>   cares,
> Washed marvellously with sorrow, swift to
>   mirth.
> The years had given them kindness. Dawn was
>   theirs,
> And sunset, and the colours of the earth.
> These had seen movement and heard music;
>   known

Slumber and waking; loved; gone proudly
    friended;
Touched flowers and furs and cheeks. All this
    is ended.

There are waters blown by changing winds to
    laughter
And lit by the rich skies, all day. And after,
Frost, with a gesture, stays the waves that dance
And wandering loveliness. He leaves a white
unbroken glory, a gathered radiance,
A width, a shining peace under the night.

                Rupert Brooke, 'The
                Dead', in *Palgrave's*
                Golden Treasury

The effects of prayer, then, are to unite us ever more closely to God and to our fellow men, whether living or dead. With this union comes an increase in the theological virtues: faith, hope and love. We grow in faith in God our Father who made and loves us, in hope that he will mould our mortal clay in his likeness, and in a love that makes us incandescent because of his life within us.

A Prayer

Almighty God and Father of us all,
Have mercy upon this troubled world of ours.
We are a pilgrim people,
Men of clay,
Captives of our own greed and frailty.
And yet,
We are the work of your hands.
You have made us in your own image
And we bear within us
Your Spirit of life,
The seeds of immortality.
Give us, we pray,
A stronger faith
So that we may walk joyously into the unknown,
An unshakeable hope
So that we may comfort the despairing,
And a love
As vast as all the oceans
So that we may hold all mankind
In our hearts.
All powerful God,
Look in your love upon us, your pilgrim people,
As we struggle towards you.
Be our food for the journey,
Our wine for rejoicing,
Our light in the darkness,
And our welcome at the journey's end.

Acknowledgements

The author is grateful to use the following material:

Caryll Houselander, *A Rocking Horse Catholic*, Sheed & Ward, 1960
Christopher Jones, *Listen Pilgrim*, Darton Longman & Todd, 1968